Daily Math
Warm-Ups
Grade One

by
M.J. Owen

Carson-Dellosa Publishing Company, Inc.
Greensboro, North Carolina

Credits

Editors
Hank Rudisill
Amy Gamble

Cover Design
Dez Perrotti

Cover Photo
EyeWire Images

Layout Design
Hank Rudisill

Art Coordinator
Betsy Peninger

Artists
Jon Nawrocik
Julie Kinlaw
Mike Duggins
Courtney Bunn
Erik Huffine

ISBN 0-88724-817-9

Table of Contents
Daily Math Warm-Ups Grade One

Introduction to *Daily Math Warm-Ups*

Based on standards specified by the National Council of Teachers of Mathematics (NCTM), *Daily Math Warm-Ups* will give teachers a year-long collection of challenging problems that reinforce math skills taught in the classroom. Designed around the traditional school year, the series offers 180 daily lessons (sets of five problems each) including computation, graph, and word problems. For each two-week group of lessons, an eight-problem multiple-choice assessment is provided to help you easily identify which students have mastered which concepts. The daily practice will help improve students' skills and bolster their confidence.

How to Use This Book

You can use this book in the following ways:
- Use the problems as a daily math warm-up. Make each child responsible for keeping a math journal which is checked periodically. Copy the daily lessons on transparencies. At the beginning of each class, put the problems on an overhead and give students approximately five minutes to solve the problems. When students have completed the exercise, go over the problems as a class. You can use this opportunity to discuss why some answers are correct and others are not.
- Because copying from the board or overhead is challenging for some learners, you may choose to photocopy the daily lessons for particular students, or for the entire class. Have students work on the problems at the beginning of class, then continue as described above.
- Give each student a copy of the problems near the end of class and have them turn the work in as a "Ticket Out the Door." You can then check students' work and then return their work and go over the answers at the beginning of the next class period.

Daily Math Warm-Ups includes many elements that will help students master a wide range of mathematical concepts. These include:

- 180 five-problem lessons based on standards specified by the National Council of Teachers of Mathematics

- 18 multiple-choice assessment tests in standardized-test format, to help identify concepts mastered and concepts in need of reteaching

- 12 real-world application extension activities

- A reproducible problem-solving strategy guide for students (on the inside back cover)

- Plenty of computation, graph, and word-problem solving opportunities that become more difficult as students progress through the school year

Lesson 1

1. $7 + 2 =$

2. Maggie picks 6 flowers. Her mom gives her 2 more flowers. How many flowers does Maggie have now?

    Maggie has _____ flowers now.

3. How many dots are there?

    There are _____ dots.

4. $4 + 8 =$

5. $3 + 6 =$

Lesson 2

1. Put the numbers in order from least to greatest.
    2, 5, 8, 1

    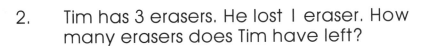

2. Tim has 3 erasers. He lost 1 eraser. How many erasers does Tim have left?

    Tim has _____ erasers left.

3. $6 + 4 =$

4. $9 + 3 =$

5. Look at the bar graph. How many books did Ken read in March?

    Ken read _____ books in March.

Books Read by Ken

Lesson 3

1. Look at the picture graph. How many days did it rain during Week 3?

   It rained _____ days during Week 3.

2. $9 + 9 =$

3. Circle the number that is greatest.

   3   5   10   1

4. $10 + 0 =$

5. Patrick has 3 blue shirts. If he gets 1 more blue shirt as a birthday present, how many blue shirts does Patrick have now? Write the number sentence and solve the problem on the line below.

   _____

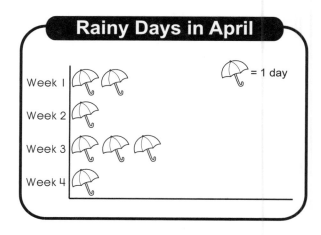

Rainy Days in April

Week 1
Week 2
Week 3
Week 4

= 1 day

Lesson 4

1. Ben checks out 5 books at the library. Later, he checks out 2 more books. How many books does Ben have now? Write the number sentence and solve the problem on the line below.

   _____

2. Circle the number that is least.

   2   12   5   6

3. $4 + 6 =$

4. $3 + 7 =$

5. Look at the bar graph. Write the title of the graph on the line below.

   _____

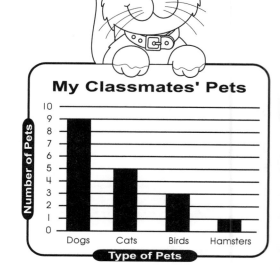

My Classmates' Pets

Number of Pets

10
9
8
7
6
5
4
3
2
1
0

Dogs   Cats   Birds   Hamsters

Type of Pets

Lesson 5

1. Look at the picture graph. How many hours did Joan spend eating?

   Joan spent _____ hours eating.

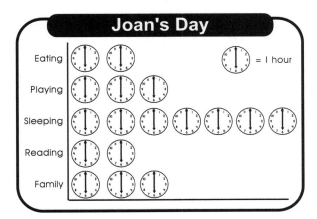

2. 2 + 2 =

3. 8 + 7 =

4. 1 + 3 =

5. Put the following numbers in order from least to greatest.
   12, 14, 16, 13, 15

   _____, _____, _____, _____, _____

Lesson 6

1. Circle the number that is greatest.

   23   32   28   22

2. Will caught 4 fish on Saturday morning. Later that day, he caught 7 more fish. How many fish did Will catch in all?

   Will caught _____ fish in all.

3. 10 + 10 =

4. 9 + 5 =

5. 2 + 8 =

Lesson 7

1. Look at the picture graph. How many people have brothers?

    _____ people have brothers.

2. Matt ate 3 cupcakes after lunch and 2 cupcakes after dinner. How many cupcakes did Matt eat in all?

    Matt ate _____ cupcakes in all.

3. Put the following numbers in order from least to greatest.
    0, 10, 9, 17

    _____, _____, _____, _____

4. 5 + 5 =

5. Draw 3 balloons in the box.

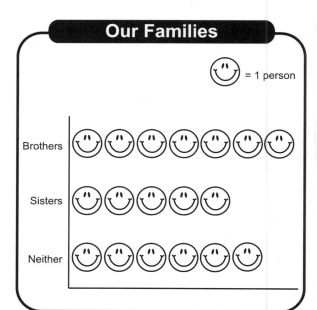

Our Families

 = 1 person

Brothers

Sisters

Neither

Lesson 8

1. 8 + 8 =

2. 9 + 2 =

3. Circle the number that is least.   14   41

4. If Darrel has 11 baseball cards and trades for 5 more, how many cards does Darrel have now? Write the number sentence and solve the problem on the line below.

    _____

5. Look at the bar graph. How many students like chocolate ice cream best?
    _____ students like chocolate ice cream best.

Favorite Ice Cream Flavors

Number of Students

Chocolate Vanilla Strawberry Mint

Flavor

Lesson 9

1. Circle the key to the picture graph.

2. $7 + 8 =$

3. $5 + 9 =$

4. Circle the number that is greater.

   58   82

5. If 6 bees are building a hive and 3 more bees come to help, how many bees are now building the hive? Write the number sentence and solve the problem on the line below.

Number of Phone Calls

= 1 call

Monday

Tuesday

Wednesday

Thursday

Friday

Lesson 10

1. Ella did 7 pages of math homework on Monday and 3 more pages of math homework on Tuesday. How many pages of math homework did Ella do on Monday and Tuesday combined? Write the number sentence and solve the problem on the line below.

   _____

2. $9 + 6 =$

3. $10 + 7 =$

4. $8 - 7 =$

5. Circle the number that is greater than 17 but less than 20.

   17   18   20   21

Lesson 11

1. Circle the number in the tens place. **4 5**

2. Draw the next shape in the pattern.

3. Draw a picture in the box that shows 12 flowers.

4. $10 + 9 =$

5. $3 + 2 =$

Lesson 12

1. Write each word in the correct column of the table.
   six, red, blue, four, three, orange, zero

2. Brianna drives 8 miles on Saturday to get to the grocery store. On Sunday, she drives 9 miles to get to the mall. How many miles did Brianna drive in all?

   Brianna drove _____ miles in all.

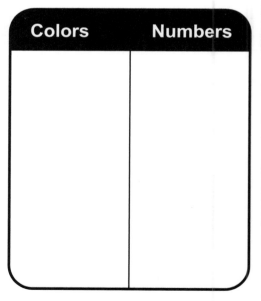

Colors	Numbers

3. $2 + 3 =$

4. $8 + 10 =$

5. $5 + 5 =$

Lesson 13

1. Fill in the blank to complete the pattern.
   1, 2, 3, 4, 5, _____, 7, 8

2. $4 + 10 =$

3. What number do the Base Ten Blocks show? _____

4. Terri has 3 CDs. She buys 2 new CDs at the store. Circle the operation sign you would use to find the number of CDs Terri has in all.

   +   **X**   **—**

5. $1 + 2 =$

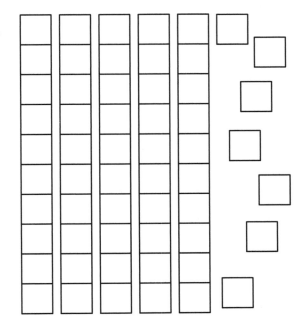

Lesson 14

1. Look at the number line. Is the number 12 closer to 10 or to 20?

   Circle the answer: 10   20

2. $9 + 10 =$

3. $5 + 2 =$

4. $10 + 3 =$

5. Chris and Frank want to share 10 cookies equally. Draw a picture in the box to show how many cookies each boy will get.

Lesson 15

1. The circle is divided into how many equal parts?

   _____

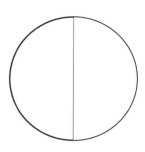

2. $3 + 9 =$

3. Cliff has 9 apples. He gives away 3 apples. Draw a picture in the box to show the number sentence $9 - 3 =$.

4. $10 + 10 =$

5. $4 + 6 =$

Lesson 16

1. How many cupcakes do not have candles? How many cupcakes are there in all? Write the answers in the blanks.

   _____ of the _____
   cupcakes do not have
   candles.

2. $6 + 5 =$

3. $15 - 8 =$

4. $1 + 8 =$

5. Circle the correct word and write it in the blank.
   When you take things away, you _____ .

   add   subtract   multiply

Lesson 17

1. 6 + 6 =

2. Write the next letter in the pattern. Z, A, Z, B, Z, C, Z, _____, Z, E, Z, F, Z, G

3. Jake had 10 balls. He lost 7 balls. How many balls does Jake have left?
    Draw a picture in the box to show your answer. Fill in the blank.
    Jake had _____ balls left.

    [blank box]

4. 5 + 1 =

5. 3 + 4 =

Lesson 18

1. On the line below, write the number sentence for this picture.

    _____

2. Mimi had 11 dolls. She gave 2 dolls to her granddaughter. How many
    dolls does Mimi have left?
    Mimi has _____ dolls left.

3. 9 – 1 =

4. 2 + 3 =

5. 9 + 10 =

Lesson 19

1. $6 + 4 =$

2. Fill in the blank to complete the pattern.
   square, rectangle, square, _____, square, rectangle

3. Use the picture to fill in the blank. $10 - 3 =$ ____.

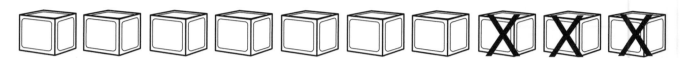

4. Kisha had 15 tomato plants in her garden. She forgot to water her plants and 8 of her tomato plants died. How many tomato plants does Kisha have now?

   Kisha has ____ tomato plants left.

5. $7 + 3 =$

Lesson 20

1. Look at the picture. How many cookies did Jane bake for her class?

   Jane baked ____ cookies for her class.

  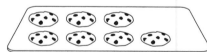

2. $9 + 6 =$

3. $9 - 7 =$

4. If 11 cups are on the table and 6 cups have straws in them, how many cups do not have straws in them?

   ____ cups do not have straws in them.

5. $2 + 6 =$

Lesson 21

1. Linda packed 3 suitcases to take on vacation. She forgot 1 suitcase. How many suitcases did Linda remember to take on vacation?

   Linda took _____ suitcases on vacation.

2. 7 + 10 =

3. Look at the picture. Is Max more likely to pull an apple or an orange out of the bag?

   Circle the answer: apple   orange

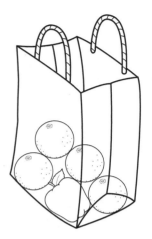

4. 2 + 9 =

5. 13 – 5 =

Lesson 22

1. Look at the picture. Pam and her friends ordered ice cream. Is it more likely that Pam ordered 1 or 2 scoops?

   Circle the answer: 1 scoop   2 scoops

2. 4 + 8 =

3. 20 – 10 =

4. Fill in the blank with a number to make the number sentence true.
   7 – _____ = 4

5. Look at the picture. If 5 trees changed color last fall, how many trees did not change color?

   _____ trees did not change color.

Lesson 23

1. Tim is thinking of some numbers. The numbers are greater than 3, but less than 7. Circle the number that Tim is not thinking of.

   1   4   5   6

2. 10 – 2 =

3. Fill in the blank with <, >, or = to make the number sentence true.
   14 _____ 19

4. Look at the picture. There are 7 dogs and 5 of the dogs have bows. How many dogs do not have bows?
   _____ dogs do not have bows.

5. 7 + 8 =

Lesson 24

1. A group of 5 students voted for their favorite color. If 3 students liked pink, 1 liked orange, and 1 liked yellow, which color did most students vote for?
   Most students voted for the color _____.

2. 4 – 3 =

3. Fill in the blank with <, >, or = to make the number sentence true.
   9 _____ 19

4. A group of 7 friends went to an amusement park. If only 3 friends bought cotton candy, how many friends did not buy cotton candy?
   _____ friends did not buy cotton candy.

5. Circle the number that is greater than 8 but less than 12.
   5   8   11   17

Name _____

Lesson 25

1. Fill in the blank with a number to make the number sentence true.

   4 + _____ + 3 = 11

2. 8 + 8 =

3. Look at the picture. Is Lee more likely to pick a pencil or a pen out of the bag?
   Circle the answer: pencil   pen

4. 9 + 5 =

5. Jon loves to take pictures. He used 10 rolls of film in June and 7 rolls of film in July. How many rolls of film total did Jon use in June and July?

   Jon used _____ rolls of film total in June and July.

Lesson 26

1. Look at the picture. If 2 pizzas do not have mushrooms and the rest of the pizzas have mushrooms, how many pizzas have mushrooms?

   _____ pizzas have mushrooms.

2. 9 – 7 =

3. Fill in the blank with a number to make the number sentence true.

   14 – _____ = 9

4. 9 + 9 =

5. Look at the picture graph. How many students like Saturday best?

   _____ students like Saturday best.

Favorite Day of the Week

✔ =1 student

Friday	✔✔✔✔✔
Saturday	✔✔✔✔✔✔✔✔
Sunday	✔✔✔

17

Daily Math Warm-Ups Grade 1

Lesson 27

1. Look at the picture. Are there more hats or socks in the bag?

   Circle the answer: hats   socks

2. $6 + 3 =$

3. Fill in the blank with <, >, or = to make the number sentence true.

   7 _____ 7

4. $8 - 2 =$

5. Meg packed 6 sandwiches for the picnic. If 3 sandwiches fell out of Meg's basket, how many sandwiches does Meg have left?

   Meg has _____ sandwiches left.

Lesson 28

1. Look at the picture. What number is Antonio most likely to spin using this spinner?

   _____

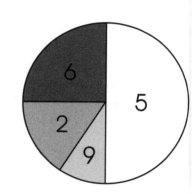

2. $8 - 7 =$

3. Fill in the blank with <, >, or = to make the number sentence true.

   15 _____ 5

4. $9 - 3 =$

5. There are 14 boxes on a shelf. If 5 of the boxes are pink, how many of the boxes are not pink?

   _____ of the boxes on the shelf are not pink.

Lesson 29

1. Look at the picture. Out of 7 boys total, 5 boys have on long pants. How many boys have on shorts?

   _____ boys have on shorts.

2. $16 - 8 =$

3. Fill in the blank with a number to make the number sentence true.
   $7 +$ _____ $+ 2 = 13$

4. $4 + 4 =$

5. There are 2 tables in the classroom. Each table has 4 books on it. How many books total are there on the 2 tables?

   There are _____ books total on the 2 tables.

Lesson 30

1. Look at the picture. May owns 1 of these pets. Based on the picture, is it more likely May owns a dog or cat?

   It is more likely May owns a _____.

2. $9 + 4 =$

3. Fill in the blank with a number to make the number sentence true.
   $2 +$ _____ $+ 5 = 10$

4. Lee bought 15 stamps. He used 10 stamps. How many stamps does Lee have left?

   Lee has _____ stamps left.

5. Circle the number that is least.

   0   10   2   16

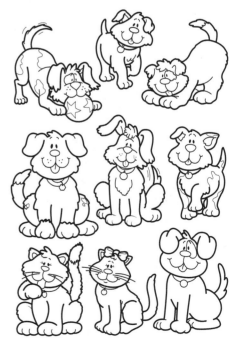

Lesson 31

1. Draw circles around the dots to show 4 equal groups.

2. $2 + 2 =$

3. $30 + 10 =$

4. $7 - 3 =$

5. Jack swam for 3 hours on Saturday and 4 hours on Sunday. How many hours did Jack swim on Saturday and Sunday combined?

   Jack swam _____ hours on Saturday and Sunday combined.

Lesson 32

1. $10 + 4 =$

2. Draw one line of symmetry through the triangle.

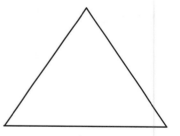

3. $20 + 50 =$

4. Molly has to be at her piano lesson at 4 o'clock. Draw hands showing 4 o'clock on the clock.

5. $4 - 1 =$

Lesson 33

1. Draw a heart in the box. Then, draw one line of symmetry through the heart.

2. 8 + 7 =

3. 18 − 9 =

4. 30 + 30 =

5. Latonya buys 12 gallons of lemonade for the party. She serves 9 gallons of lemonade during the party. How many gallons of lemonade does Latonya have left?

   Latonya has _____ gallons of lemonade left.

Lesson 34

1. What is the name of this shape? _____

   How many sides does this shape have? _____

   How many corners? _____

2. 1 + 15 =

3. 11 + 9 =

4. 17 − 8 =

5. Otto plants 10 bushes one day and 6 bushes the next. How many bushes did Otto plant in all?

   Otto planted _____ bushes in all.

Lesson 35

1. $13 - 6 =$

2. Circle the shape that shows a line of symmetry.

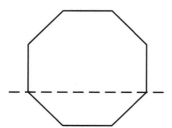 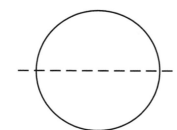 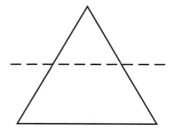

3. $8 + 8 =$

4. Jesse orders 2 chocolate shakes and 6 ice cream cones at the Ice Cream Shop. How many chocolate shakes and ice cream cones does Jesse order in all?

    Jesse orders _____ chocolate shakes and ice cream cones in all.

5. $20 + 5 =$

Lesson 36

1. What is the total of the lengths of the sides of the triangle?

    _____ + _____ + _____ = _____ inches

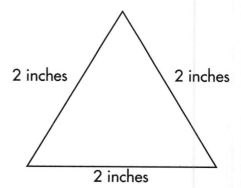

2 inches   2 inches

2 inches

2. $23 - 3 =$

3. $16 - 9 =$

4. $18 + 2 =$

5. Dominic has 3 pillows and 8 stuffed animals on his bed. How many more stuffed animals than pillows does Dominic have?

    Dominic has _____ more stuffed animals than pillows.

Lesson 37

1. Look at the map. Circle the house that is closest to city hall.

2. $6 - 2 =$

3. Jerry drew 19 triangles and 5 squares. How many more triangles than squares did Jerry draw?

   Jerry drew _____ more triangles than squares.

4. $10 - 3 =$

5. $50 + 50 =$

Lesson 38

1. $19 - 9 =$

2. $80 + 20 =$

3. Circle the shape that has fewer than 4 sides.

4. $21 - 1 =$

5. Tracy has to be at soccer practice at 5 o'clock. Draw hands on the clock to show what time Tracy has to be at soccer practice.

Lesson 39

1. 13 + 6 =

2. 28 − 8 =

3. Circle the shape that looks most like your math book.

  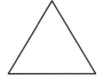

4. Adam has 16 apples in one bag and 10 oranges in another bag. How many apples and oranges does Adam have in both bags?

    Adam has _____ apples and oranges in both bags.

5. 12 + 5 =

Lesson 40

1. Sarah bought 2 pounds of red grapes and 3 pounds of green grapes at the grocery store. How many pounds of red and green grapes did Sarah buy altogether?

    Sarah bought _____ pounds of red and green grapes.

2. 17 + 2 =

3. 15 − 3 =

4. 7 + 2 =

5. Look at the picture. The scale measures pounds. How much does the book weigh?

    The book weighs _____ pounds.

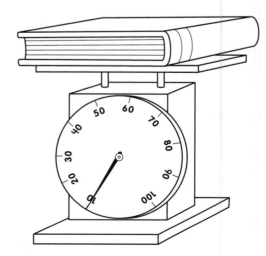

Lesson 41

Estimate. Circle the best answer for problems 1 through 3.

1. $9 + 10 =$
   9   10   20

2. $21 + 12 =$
   20   30   40

3. $13 + 17 =$
   10   15   30

Number of Zoo Visitors

4. Look at the bar graph. On which day did the zoo have the most visitors?

   The zoo had the most visitors on _____.

5. Tara worked 10 hours on Monday and 8 hours on Tuesday. How many hours did Tara work in all?

   Tara worked _____ hours in all.

Lesson 42

1. $9 + 7 =$

2. $6 + 4 =$

3. $7 + 7 =$

4. Look at the tally chart. Chelsea asked her classmates whether they liked chocolate milk or white milk best. How many classmates does Chelsea have in all?
   Chelsea has _____ classmates.

Chocolate	White
‖‖ ‖‖ ‖‖	‖‖	

5. Jason has 11 games. If he buys 4 more games, how many games will Jason have in all?

   Jason will have _____ games in all.

Lesson 43

1. Look at the tally chart. How many more people like purple best than like orange best?

   _____ more people like purple best.

Favorite Color

Orange	Purple	Yellow
|||	┼┼┼ ||	┼┼┼

2. $15 - 4 =$

3. $12 - 9 =$

4. $9 - 3 =$

5. Peggy checks out 13 books at the library. She returns 6 of the books early. How many books does Peggy still have?

   Peggy still has _____ books checked out from the library.

Lesson 44

1. $15 + 5 =$

2. $30 - 20 =$

3. $45 - 5 =$

4. Sam had 30 baseball cards. His little sister gave him 4 more baseball cards. How many baseball cards does Sam have now?

   Sam now has _____ baseball cards.

5. Look at the tally chart. Based on the information, what color hair do more people have?

   More people have _____ hair.

Hair Color

Brown	Black	Red	Blonde
┼┼┼ |||	┼┼┼ |	||||	|||

Lesson 45

1. Look at the picture graph. How many goals were scored in July and August?

   _____ goals were scored in July and August.

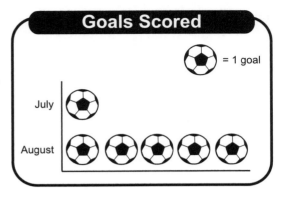

2. 19 – 6 =

3. 13 – 12 =

4. 25 + 5 =

5. There are 70 students in first grade. If 10 students leave during the school year, how many students are left at the end of the school year?

   _____ students are left at the end of the school year.

Lesson 46

1. Juan has 4 new shirts and 2 of his new shirts are striped. How many of Juan's new shirts do not have stripes? Draw a picture in the box to show your answer. Then, fill in the blank.

   _____ of Juan's new shirts do not have stripes.

For 2 through 4, fill in the blank with <, >, or = to make each number sentence true.

2. 38 _____ 23

3. 19 _____ 16

4. 29 _____ 44

5. 40 + 10 =

Lesson 47

1. Tony is reading a book that has 20 pages. He has read 10 pages. How many pages does Tony have left to read?

   Tony has _____ pages left to read.

For 2 through 4, fill in the blank to make each number sentence true.

2. $5 +$ _____ $+ 5 = 20$

3. $6 + 1 + 2 =$ _____

4. $2 +$ _____ $+ 11 = 13$

5. What time is shown on the clock?

   _____ o'clock

Lesson 48

1. Oliver buys 16 T-shirts at the ball game. He gives away 8 T-shirts. How many T-shirts does he have left?

   Oliver has _____ T-shirts left.

2. Circle the group that is greater.

 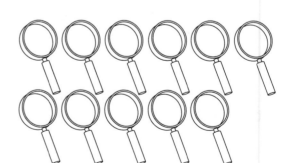

3. $90 + 20 =$

4. $10 - 3 =$

5. $30 - 10 =$

Lesson 49

Name _____

1. How many more ice cream cones are shown in Box #1 than in Box #2?
   _____ more ice cream cones are shown in Box #1 than Box #2.

Box #1

Box #2

2. 27 − 6 =

3. 14 + 4 =

4. 17 − 9 =

5. Ling has some marbles in her pocket. If 8 marbles are red and 12 marbles are black, how many red and black marbles does Ling have? Ling has _____ red and black marbles.

Lesson 50

1. Circle the shape that completes the pattern.

For 2 through 4, fill in the blank to make each number sentence true.

2. 7 + 8 + _____ = 17

3. 4 + 9 + _____ = 19

4. 3 + _____ + 9 = 16

5. Tasha invites 13 friends to her slumber party. If 2 of her friends can't come, how many friends are able to come to Tasha's slumber party? _____ friends are able to come to Tasha's slumber party.

© Carson-Dellosa CD-7425   29   *Daily Math Warm-Ups Grade 1*

Lesson 51

1. Paris has 6 brothers and 5 sisters. How many brothers and sisters does Paris have in all?

   Paris has _____ brothers and sisters in all.

2. How many paper clips long is the pencil?

   The pencil is _____ paper clips long.

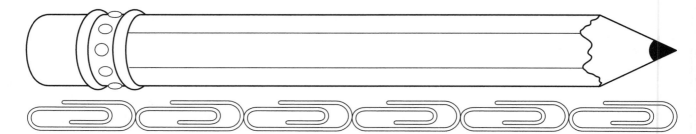

3. $7 + 10 =$

4. $14 - 8 =$

5. $10 + 90 =$

Lesson 52

1. Circle the square that shows a correctly drawn line of symmetry.

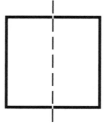 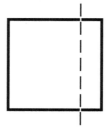

2. Mary runs 5 miles on Tuesday and 3 miles on Thursday. How many miles did Mary run on Tuesday and Thursday combined?

   Mary ran _____ miles on Tuesday and Thursday.

3. $15 - 1 =$

4. $16 - 10 =$

5. What time is shown on the clock? _____ o'clock

Lesson 53

1. Hayley read 7 books in one month. She read 9 books the next month. How many books did Hayley read in all?

    Hayley read _____ books in all.

2. What time is shown on the clock? _____ o'clock

3. 5 + 7 =

4. 28 − 8 =

5. 40 + 30 =

Lesson 54

1. Pete helped his mom wash the dishes. He washed 8 plates, 4 bowls, and 6 cups. How many plates, bowls, and cups did Pete wash?

    Pete washed _____ plates, bowls, and cups.

2. 16 + 3 =

3. 70 + 5 =

4. 22 − 1 =

5. Look at the picture graph. Complete the graph by drawing the correct number of gum balls sold each day. Then, answer the question. How many gum balls were sold on Saturday?

    _____ gum balls were sold on Saturday.

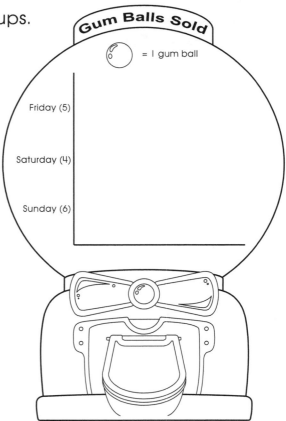

Gum Balls Sold

= 1 gum ball

Friday (5)

Saturday (4)

Sunday (6)

Lesson 55

1. Gwen's house is 6 miles from the school. The school is 9 more miles from the store. How many miles is Gwen's house from the store?

 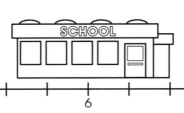 

Gwen's house is _____ miles from the store.

2. 10 + 70 =

3. 70 – 10 =

4. 33 – 3 =

5. Read the clues. Draw the mystery shape in the box. Clues: I have no sides and no corners. I am round.

Lesson 56

1. Ingrid had 17 hamsters. If 3 hamsters ran away, how many hamsters does Ingrid have now?

Ingrid has _____ hamsters.

2. 16 + 3 =

3. 6 + 13 =

4. 3 + 12 =

5. Circle the square.

 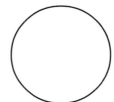 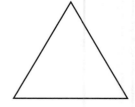

Lesson 57

1. There are 15 umbrellas by the front door. If 7 umbrellas are red and the rest are yellow, how many of the umbrellas are yellow?

   _____ of the umbrellas are yellow.

2. $22 + 10 =$

3. $25 - 10 =$

4. $11 + 9 =$

5. How many inches long is the eraser?

   The eraser is _____ inches long.

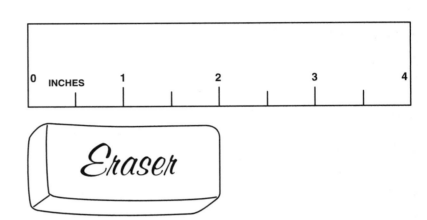

Lesson 58

1. Jan had 17 pieces of candy. She gave away 8 pieces of candy. How many pieces of candy does Jan have left?

   Jan has _____ pieces of candy left.

2. $17 - 3 =$

3. $12 + 6 =$

4. $15 + 4 =$

5. How many books long is the table?

   The table is _____ books long.

Lesson 59

1. Kayla has 4 brown beads, 9 yellow beads, and 2 purple beads. How many brown, yellow, and purple beads does she have altogether?

   Kayla has ____ brown, yellow, and purple beads altogether.

2. 2 + 20 =

3. 20 – 2 =

4. 14 + 10 =

5. Circle the shape below that has 4 corners.

Lesson 60

1. At the fair, 15 kids ordered strawberry ice cream and 4 kids ordered vanilla ice cream. How many more kids ordered strawberry ice cream than vanilla ice cream?

   _____ more kids ordered strawberry ice cream than vanilla ice cream?

2. 5 – 4 =

3. 18 + 2 =

4. 26 – 5 =

5. Rory's mom tells him to be home at 12:00. Circle the clock that shows the time Rory has to be home.

Lesson 61

1. It rained 4 inches on Thursday and 2 inches on Friday. How much more did it rain on Thursday than Friday?

    It rained _____ more inches on Thursday than on Friday.

2. 12 – 8 =

3. 21 – 1 =

4. 2 + 15 =

5. Count the number of boys and the number of girls in your class. Record your information in the tally chart.

Boys/Girls in Class	
Boys	Girls

Lesson 62

1. Winnie went to the store. She bought 3 grapefruit, 6 apples, and 4 oranges. How many pieces of fruit did Winnie buy in all?

    Winnie bought _____ pieces of fruit.

2. 20 + 9 =

3. 17 – 9 =

4. 18 + 0 =

5. Look at the bar graph. How many more hours were spent on homework on Thursday than on Tuesday?

    _____ more hours were spent on homework on Thursday.

Time Spent on Homework

Lesson 63

1. Look at the picture graph. How many more books did Cari read in July than in August?

   Cari read _____ more books in July.

2. $70 - 50 =$

3. $10 + 10 =$

4. $17 + 3 =$

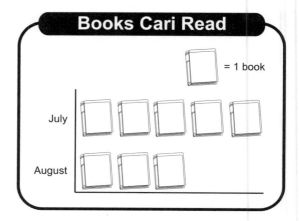

Books Cari Read

= 1 book

July

August

5. Amy has 10 pencils in one school box and 6 pencils in another school box. How many pencils does Amy have in both school boxes combined?

   Amy has _____ pencils in both school boxes.

Lesson 64

1. Look at the bar graph. Who has the most pennies in her piggy bank?

   _____ has the most pennies in her piggy bank.

2. $9 + 13 =$

3. $13 - 9 =$

4. $35 + 10 =$

5. Draw the next picture in the pattern.

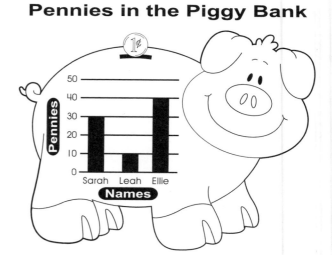

Pennies in the Piggy Bank

Pennies

50 40 30 20 10 0

Sarah   Leah   Ellie

Names

Lesson 65

1. Look at the picture graph. How many more miles did Joe bike on Saturday than on Sunday?

   Joe biked _____ more miles on Saturday than on Sunday.

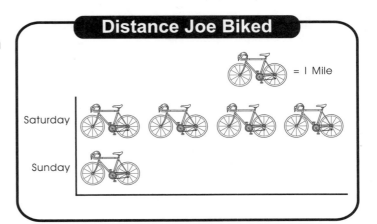

Distance Joe Biked

= 1 Mile

Saturday

Sunday

2. $40 - 20 =$

3. $17 - 8 =$

4. $5 + 12 =$

5. Andre crossed 13 streets on his way to school and 11 streets on his way home. How many streets did Andre cross in all?

   Andre crossed _____ streets in all.

Lesson 66

1. Draw the next shape in the pattern.

       _____

2. $4 + 9 =$

3. $14 - 9 =$

4. Jackie put 9 blocks in a pile. Later, she added 10 blocks. How many blocks did Jackie put in the pile?

   Jackie put _____ blocks in the pile.

5. Look at the bar graph. How many more bricks are in Pile 2 than in Pile 1?

   There are _____ more bricks in Pile 2 than in Pile 1.

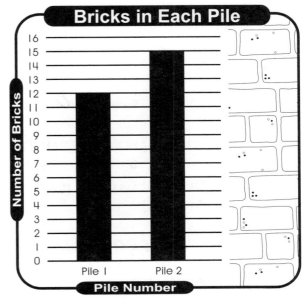

Bricks in Each Pile

Number of Bricks

16 15 14 13 12 11 10 9 8 7 6 5 4 3 2 1 0

Pile 1   Pile 2

Pile Number

Lesson 67

1. Look at the bar graph. Which class has the most students?

   Class _____ has the most students.

2. 20 – 10 =

3. 21 + 7 =

4. 16 + 1 =

5. There are 10 squirrels and 15 birds in a tree. How many animals are in the tree in all?

   There are _____ animals in the tree in all.

Students in Each Class

Lesson 68

1. Terri made 20 ham sandwiches and 6 turkey sandwiches for the campers. How many sandwiches did Terri make in all?

   Terri made _____ sandwiches.

2. 16 – 5 =

3. 9 + 3 =

4. 10 + 40 =

5. Look at the picture graph. How many more people like caramel candy than chocolate candy?

   _____ more people like caramel candy than chocolate candy.

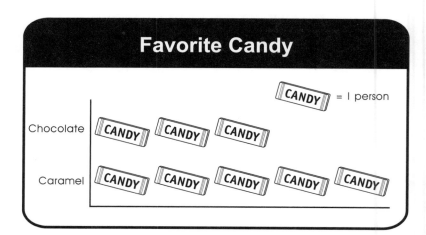

Favorite Candy

Lesson 69

1. $1 + 3 =$

2. $15 - 7 =$

3. $16 - 8 =$

4. Look at the bar graph. How many more snowy days were there in January than in March?

   There were _____ more snowy days in January than in March.

5. In Ray's class, 10 students prefer spring and 18 prefer fall. How many more students prefer fall?

   _____ more people prefer fall.

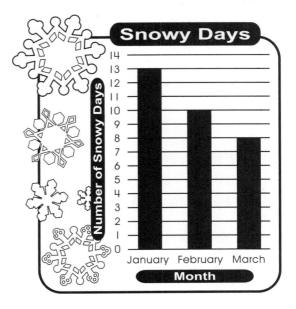

Lesson 70

1. Look at the picture graph. How many more blue cars were on the road than red cars?

   _____ more blue cars were on the road than red cars.

2. Anna has 22 markers and 2 crayons. How many more markers than crayons does Anna have?

   Anna has _____ more markers.

3. $28 - 7 =$

4. $13 - 8 =$

5. $60 + 40 =$

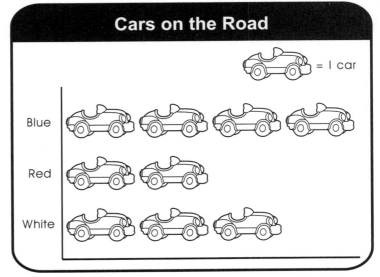

Lesson 71

1. $19 + 9 =$

2.   What number do the Base Ten Blocks show?

3.   Jamal had 30 comic books. He gave away 10. How many comic books does Jamal have left?

   Jamal has _____ comic books left.

4. $15 - 9 =$

5. $12 + 8 =$

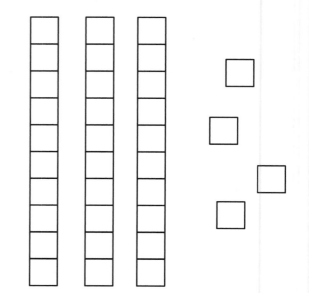

Lesson 72

1.   On field day, the first graders ordered 10 sausage pizzas and 9 cheese pizzas. How many pizzas did the first graders order in all?

   The first graders ordered _____ pizzas.

2. $17 - 6 =$

3. $4 + 30 =$

4. $12 - 6 =$

5.   Look at the bar graph. How many more hours of television did Melissa watch than Hap?

   Melissa watched _____ more hours of television than Hap.

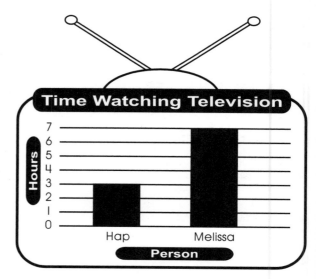

Lesson 73

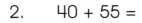

Name _____

1. Sarah and Kassie want to share 10 books equally. How many books will each girl get?

   Each girl will get _____ books.

2. $40 + 55 =$

3. $25 - 4 =$

4. $14 + 6 =$

5. Look at the picture. How many bricks tall is the boy?

   The boy is _____ bricks tall.

Lesson 74

1. How many centimeters long is the barrette?

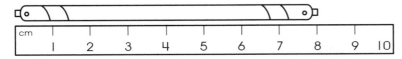

   The barrette is _____ centimeters long.

2. Look at the picture graph. How many more children like pepperoni pizza than mushroom pizza?

   _____ more children like pepperoni pizza.

3. $13 - 9 =$

4. $14 + 5 =$

5. $80 + 5 =$

Favorite Pizza

= 1 child

Pepperoni

Mushroom

Cheese

Name _____

Lesson 75

1. Look at the bar graph. How many elephants and monkeys are in the zoo?

   _____ elephants and monkeys are in the zoo.

Animals in Zoo

2. 60 + 30 =

3. 60 − 60 =

4. 9 + 8 =

5. Look at the picture. How many cookies did the girls bake altogether?

   The girls baked _____ cookies.

Lesson 76

1. Look at the picture graph. How many more medium-sized dogs live on Hay Street than large dogs?

   _____ more medium-sized dogs than large dogs live on Hay Street.

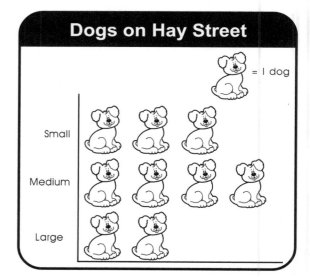

Dogs on Hay Street

= 1 dog

Small

Medium

Large

2. 7 + 7 =

3. 19 − 6 =

4. 40 + 10 =

5. Taylor has 9 dictionaries on his bookshelf. If 4 dictionaries have blue covers, how many of Taylor's dictionaries do not have blue covers?

   _____ of Taylor's dictionaries do not have blue covers.

Lesson 77

1. Draw a shape in the blank to complete the pattern.

    _____

2. Jess takes 13 jugs of water to soccer practice. The team drinks 9 jugs of water. How many jugs of water does Jess have left?

   Jess has ____ jugs of water left.

3. 50 + 20 =

4. 17 – 4 =

5. 10 – 4 =

Lesson 78

1. Fill in the blanks with numbers to complete this fact family.

   2 + 7 = _____   7 + _____ = 9

   9 – 2 = _____   9 – _____ = 2

2. Delia goes to the grocery store. She buys 14 peaches. If 7 peaches are ripe and ready to eat, how many peaches are not ready to eat?

   _____ peaches are not ready to eat.

3. 28 + 1 =

4. 19 – 6 =

5. 15 – 7 =

Lesson 79

1. Some friends go out to dinner. If 9 friends sit at one table and 11 friends sit at another table, how many friends are at both tables?

   There are _____ friends at both tables.

2. $22 + 6 =$

3. $16 - 3 =$

4. $18 - 5 =$

5. Look at the bar graph. How many people like chocolate and cream doughnuts best?

   _____ people like chocolate and cream doughnuts best.

Lesson 80

1. $35 + 5 =$

2. $17 - 7 =$

3. $9 + 8 =$

4. Fill in the blanks to complete the pattern.

   10, 12, 14, 16, _____, _____, 22

5. Hal's job is to try different ice cream flavors. He tastes 30 ice cream flavors on Monday and 20 ice cream flavors on Tuesday. How many flavors of ice cream total does Hal try on Monday and Tuesday?

   Hal tries _____ flavors of ice cream on Monday and Tuesday.

44

Lesson 81

1. Look at the bar graph. How many movies did Erik watch during July and August?

   Erik watched _____ movies during July and August.

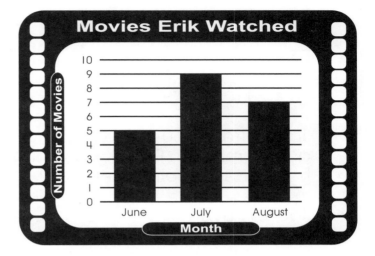

Movies Erik Watched

2. 64 – 10 =

3. 30 + 6 =

4. 21 – 1 =

5. Rashanda has 16 keys on her key ring. If 9 of the keys on her key ring belong to her brother, how many of the keys on her key ring belong to Rashanda?

   _____ of the keys belong to Rashanda.

Lesson 82

1. Brett has 28 toy cars. He gives away 8 of his cars. How many toy cars does Brett have left?

   Brett has _____ toy cars left.

2. 34 – 4 =

3. 4 + 9 =

4. 6 – 4 =

5. Look at the picture graph. How many bags of trash were collected during all 3 weeks combined?

   There were _____ bags of trash collected during all 3 weeks combined.

Bags of Trash Collected

= 1 bag

Week 1
Week 2
Week 3

Lesson 83

1. 19 − 10 =

2. 55 + 10 =

3. 70 + 20 =

4. Jacob travels 60 miles on Monday and 30 miles on Friday. How many miles does Jacob travel in all?

    Jacob travels _____ miles in all.

5. Look at the bar graph. How many more birds visited the birdbath on Tuesday than Monday?

Birds at Birdbath

_____ more birds visited the birdbath on Tuesday than on Monday.

Lesson 84

1. 15 + 5 =

2. 68 − 10 =

3. 14 − 6 =

4. Mary collects stamps. She has 91 stamps. She gives 10 stamps to her sister. How many stamps does Mary have now?

    Mary has _____ stamps now.

5. Fill in the blanks with numbers to complete this fact family.

    8 + 5 = 13   _____ + _____ = _____

    _____ − _____ = _____   _____ − _____ = _____

Lesson 85

1. Robyn makes 30 phone calls on Saturday and 4 phone calls on Sunday. How many phone calls total did Robyn make on Saturday and Sunday?

   Robyn made _____ phone calls total on Saturday and Sunday.

2. $35 - 2 =$

3. $25 + 25 =$

4. $15 - 5 =$

5. Look at the picture graph. How many people like grape and orange lollipops best?

   _____ people like grape and orange lollipops best.

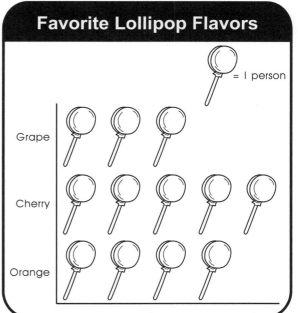

Favorite Lollipop Flavors

= 1 person

Grape

Cherry

Orange

Lesson 86

1. Fill in the blanks with numbers to complete this fact family.

   _____ + _____ = _____   _____ + _____ = _____

   $8 - 3 = 5$ _____ − _____ = _____

2. $16 - 7 =$

3. $45 - 5 =$

4. Alex buys 3 computer games one week and 5 computer games the next week. How many computer games did Alex buy in all?

   Alex bought _____ computer games in all.

5. $39 - 1 =$

Lesson 87

1. $10 + 9 =$

2. $14 - 5 =$

3. $12 - 9 =$

4. Look at the picture graph. How many runs did Tina score during April and May?

    Tina scored _____ runs during April and May.

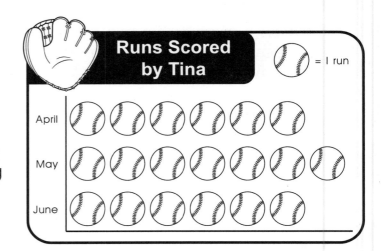

5. Pam has 7 baseball cards. She gets 11 more baseball cards over the weekend. How many baseball cards does Pam have now? Write the number sentence and solve the problem on the line below.

    _____

Lesson 88

1. $4 + 7 =$

2. $6 - 6 =$

3. $7 + 5 =$

4. Look at the bar graph. How many times did June, Carol, and Andy visit the zoo altogether?

    June, Carol, and Andy visited the zoo _____ times altogether.

5. Raul sold 30 cherry pops and 40 strawberry pops on a hot summer day. How many cherry and strawberry pops did Raul sell in all?

    Raul sold _____ cherry and strawberry pops in all.

Lesson 89

1. Look at the bar graph. How many more pages did Ashley read than Chris?

   Ashley read _____ more pages.

2. Justin rented 20 videos. He returned 10 videos on time. He returned the rest of the videos late. How many videos did Justin return late?

   Justin returned _____ videos late.

3. 55 + 3 =

4. 70 − 20 =

5. 60 + 30 =

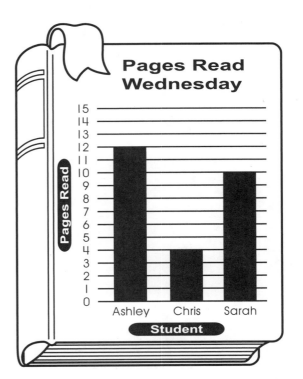

Pages Read Wednesday

Lesson 90

1. At the pet store, there are 9 dogs and 3 fish for sale. How many more dogs are for sale than fish?

   _____ more dogs are for sale than fish.

2. 19 − 9 =

3. 81 − 10 =

4. 23 + 10 =

5. Fill in the blanks to complete the fact family for these numbers. 9, 3, 6

   _____ + _____ = _____   _____ + _____ = _____

   _____ − _____ = _____   _____ − _____ = _____

Daily Math Warm-Ups Grade 1

Lesson 91

1. If 10 ducks are swimming in a pond and 7 ducks fly away, how many ducks are still swimming on the pond?

    _____ ducks are still swimming in the pond.

2. Write the number eight on the line. _____

3. $15 + 10 =$

4. $3 + 40 =$

5. $62 - 2 =$

Lesson 92

1. Cole spends 25 hours on a train. He sleeps 10 hours on the train. How many hours is Cole awake on the train?

    Cole is awake _____ hours on the train.

2. $5 - 2 =$

3. $23 + 6 =$

4. Circle the number ten.

    14   41   10   12

5. $18 - 9 =$

Lesson 93

1. Tonya buys 3 new pairs of jeans and 6 new shirts. How many new shirts and jeans does Tonya buy in all?

   Tonya buys ___ shirts and jeans in all.

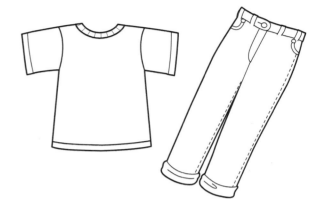

2. $15 - 6 =$

3. $13 + 5 =$

4. $20 + 5 =$

5. Put the following numbers in order from least to greatest. 15, 51, 10, 25

   _____, _____, _____, _____

Lesson 94

1. Circle the clock that shows 4:00.

2. $7 + 8 =$

3. Renee baked 15 chocolate chip cookies and 10 oatmeal cookies. How many cookies did Renee bake in all?

   Renee baked _____ cookies in all.

4. $6 - 4 =$

5. $10 - 5 =$

Lesson 95

1. 38 + 2 =

2. 25 − 3 =

3. 30 + 7 =

4. At Lynn's house there are 9 windows upstairs and 9 windows downstairs. How many windows are there in Lynn's house?
    There are _____ windows in Lynn's house.

5. Circle the clock that shows 2:30.

Lesson 96

1. 34 − 4 =

2. James has 11 flowers in a vase. If 7 flowers are orange and the rest are yellow, how many of the flowers are yellow?

    _____ of the flowers are yellow.

3. 12 − 9 =

4. 19 + 1 =

5. Tameka has seven stuffed animals in her bedroom. Circle the number seven.

    9   7   4   1

Lesson 97

1. $17 - 8 =$

2. $50 + 20 =$

3. Anna had 9¢. She spent 4¢. How much money does Anna have left?

   Anna has _____¢ left.

4. $41 + 10 =$

5. Look at the bar graph. How many people like roses more than daisies?

   _____ people like roses more than daisies.

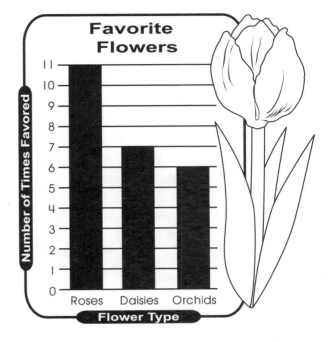

Favorite Flowers

Number of Times Favored

Flower Type: Roses, Daisies, Orchids

Lesson 98

1. $31 + 3 =$

2. $17 - 2 =$

3. Circle the clock that shows 12:30.

4. There are 16 boats at the dock. If 9 of the boats are brown and the rest are white, how many of the boats are white?
   _____ of the boats are white.

5. $25 + 5 =$

Lesson 99

1. $72 - 10 =$

2. $72 + 10 =$

3. $6 + 9 =$

4. How many centimeters long is the nail? It is _____ centimeters long.

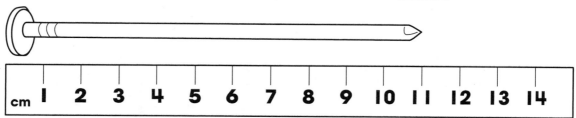

5. Out of 16 children who ate lunch, 9 ate hamburgers and the rest ate hot dogs. How many children ate hot dogs? Write the number sentence and solve the problem on the line below.

_____

Lesson 100

1. How many inches long is the pencil? It is _____ inches long.

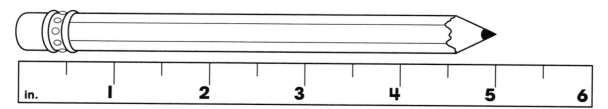

2. $6 + 3 =$

3. $7 - 1 =$

4. $20 + 40 =$

5. Angel folded 13 napkins for a party. If 5 napkins were used, how many napkins are still folded?
_____ napkins are still folded.

Lesson 101

1. Marie owns a journal with 21 pages in it. She has written on 10 pages, and the rest are blank. How many pages are still blank?

    _____ pages are still blank.

2. 10 + 2 =

3. 20 + 20 =

4. 15 − 6 =

5. Fill in the blank with <, >, or = to make the number sentence true.

    40 _____ 39

Lesson 102

1. Fill in the blank with <, >, or = to make the number sentence true.

    59 _____ 55

2. 7 + 3 =

3. 15 + 1 =

4. 19 − 2 =

5. There are 15 students in Rose's class. If 7 of the students are boys and the rest are girls, how many girls are in Rose's class?

    There are _____ girls in Rose's class.

Lesson 103

1. There are 19 shapes in a bag. If 8 of the shapes are squares and the rest are triangles, how many triangles are in the bag?

   There are _____ triangles in the bag.

2. $33 - 10 =$

3. $33 + 10 =$

4. $45 - 1 =$

5. Fill in the blank with <, >, or = to make the number sentence true.

   28 _____ 22

Lesson 104

1. Dante has 10 balloons. If 6 balloons are red and the rest are purple, how many purple balloons does Dante have?

   Dante has _____ purple balloons.

2. $37 - 10 =$

3. $14 + 5 =$

4. $10 + 80 =$

5. Look at the bar graph. How many more people picked strawberries as their favorite fruit than picked blueberries as their favorite fruit?

   _____ more people picked strawberries as their favorite fruit.

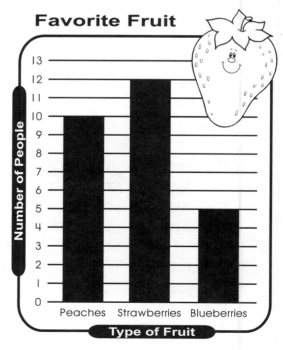

Favorite Fruit

Lesson 105

1. $19 - 7 =$

2. $18 + 3 =$

3. $19 - 5 =$

4. Look at the picture graph. How many hours total did Beth spend reading on Thursday and Saturday?

   Beth spent _____ hours reading on Thursday and Saturday.

5. Claire rode her bike 4 miles on Saturday and 5 miles on Sunday. How many miles total did Claire ride her bike?

   Claire rode her bike _____ miles total.

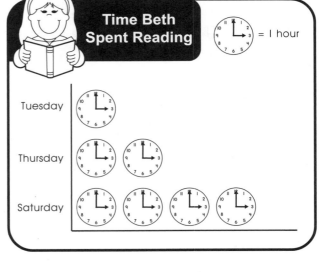

Lesson 106

1. Gigi bought 9 balloons. She gave away 4 balloons. How many balloons does Gigi have left?

   Gigi has _____ balloons left.

2. Look at the tally chart. How many more people voted for puffs than flakes as their favorite cereal?

   _____ more people voted for puffs than flakes.

3. $17 + 2 =$

4. $17 - 4 =$

5. $5 + 5 =$

Favorite Cereal

Flakes	Puffs
ǁǁǁǁ	ǁǁǁǁ
ǁǁǁǁ	ǁǁǁǁ
|||	ǁǁǁǁ

Lesson 107

1. 30 − 30 =

2. 30 + 30 =

3. Denisha invited 18 friends to her party. If 4 friends could not come, how many friends did come to Denisha's party?

   _____ friends did come to Denisha's party.

4. 4 + 1 =

5. Fill in the blank with <, >, or = to make the number sentence true.

   19 _____ 22

Lesson 108

1. 1 + 9 =

2. 90 − 10 =

3. 12 − 7 =

4. There are 18 balls in a basket. If 9 balls have stripes, how many balls do not have stripes?

   _____ balls do not have stripes.

5. Fill in the blank with + or − to make the number sentence true.

   9 _____ 3 = 12

Lesson 109

1. $13 - 5 =$

2. $14 - 6 =$

3. $16 - 8 =$

4. Look at the tally chart. How many yellow and orange buttons does Molly have altogether?

   Molly has _____ yellow and orange buttons altogether.

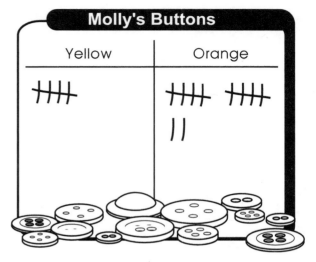

Molly's Buttons

Yellow	Orange
卌	卌 卌 ||

5. Yee went on vacation for 17 days. It rained on 7 days, but the other days were sunny. How many days were sunny?

   _____ days were sunny.

Lesson 110

1. Look at the picture graph. How many more white bunnies does Virginia have than spotted bunnies?

   _____ more white bunnies than spotted bunnies.

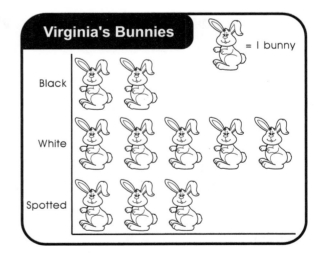

Virginia's Bunnies

= 1 bunny

Black
White
Spotted

2. $25 + 5 =$

3. $20 - 10 =$

4. $17 - 5 =$

5. Julio spent 4 hours at one baseball game and 3 hours at another. How much time did he spend at both baseball games?

   Julio spent _____ hours at both games.

Lesson 111

1. Look at the picture. How many pies did Ben bake in all?
Ben baked _____ pies in all.

2. $5 + 3 =$

3. $27 - 6 =$

4. $18 - 7 =$

5. Circle the picture that shows 2 groups of 3 eggs.

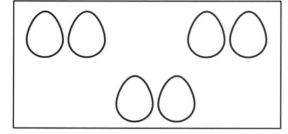 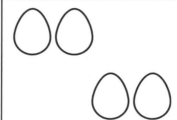 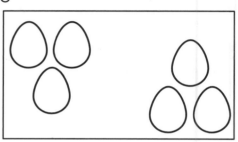

Lesson 112

1. Azur worked for 6 hours on Monday. On Tuesday, he worked 2 hours less than on Monday. How many hours did Azur work on Tuesday?
Azur worked _____ hours on Tuesday.

2. Circle the picture that shows 5 groups of 4 dots.

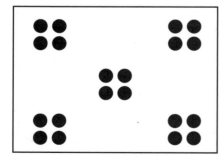 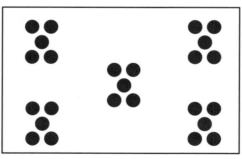 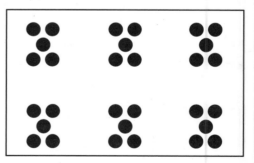

3. $30 - 10 =$

4. $3 + 3 =$

5. $12 - 4 =$

Lesson 113

1. Crystal traveled 7 hours by airplane. Then, she traveled 4 more hours by train. How many hours did Crystal travel in all?
Crystal traveled _____ hours in all.

2. Circle the picture that shows 2 groups of 2 keys.

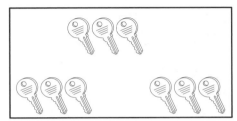  

3. $60 - 30 =$

4. $25 + 40 =$

5. $40 - 20 =$

Lesson 114

1. $17 - 8 =$

2. $21 + 4 =$

3. $16 - 7 =$

4. Liz has 2 books she wants to read. Each book has 5 pages. How many pages does Liz want to read in all?
Liz wants to read _____ pages in all.

5. Circle the picture that shows 3 groups of 4 suns.

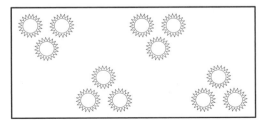 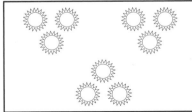 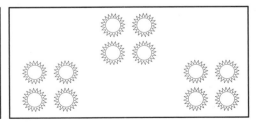

Lesson 115

1. Look at the bar graph. How many math problems were finished on Wednesday and Thursday?
_____ math problems were finished on Wednesday and Thursday.

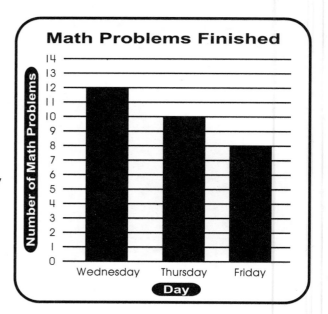

2. Kitty has 12 gum balls. She wants to share them equally between herself and her best friend, Todd. How many gum balls will each person get?
Each person will get _____ gum balls.

3. $17 - 10 =$

4. $14 + 5 =$

5. $18 - 4 =$

Lesson 116

1. $7 + 6 =$

2. John ironed 16 white shirts and 13 blue shirts. How many shirts did John iron in all?
John ironed _____ shirts in all.

3. $9 - 7 =$

4. $10 + 6 =$

5. Circle the picture that shows 5 groups of 2 squares.

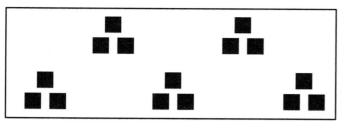
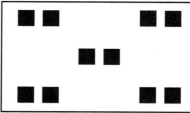
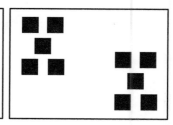

Lesson 117

1. Look at the picture graph. How many people like water best?

    _____ people prefer water.

2. 29 – 9 =

3. 11 + 8 =

4. 14 – 7 =

Favorite Drinks

Lemonade

Root Beer

Water

= 1 person

5. There are 12 boys and 11 girls in Louise's class. How many students are in Louise's class?

    There are _____ students in Louise's class.

Lesson 118

1. Mallory has 2 drawers in her dresser. Each drawer has 3 pairs of socks. How many pairs of socks are in all of the drawers?
    There are _____ pairs of socks in all of the drawers.

2. 10 – 5 =

3. 12 – 7 =

4. 6 + 10 =

5. Circle the picture that shows 5 groups of 1 sock.

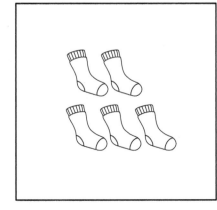
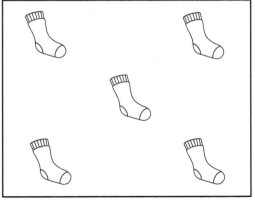
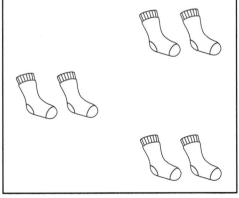

Lesson 119

1. Circle the picture that shows the number sentence 10 − 5 = .

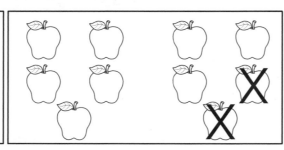 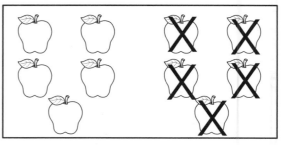

2. Wendy walked 13 blocks to school. Later, she walked 10 more blocks to swim practice. How many blocks did Wendy walk in all?
   Wendy walked _____ blocks in all.

3. 9 − 2 =

4. 5 + 11 =

5. 10 + 80 =

Lesson 120

1. How many students like vanilla or strawberry ice cream best?

   _____ children like vanilla or strawberry ice cream best.

2. 9 − 8 =

3. 14 + 5 =

4. 17 − 6 =

Favorite Ice Cream

Chocolate	Vanilla	Strawberry
卌	卌	卌
‖	卌	‖‖
	‖‖‖	

5. Kelsey has 13 blue markers and 12 green markers in her desk. How many blue and green markers does Kelsey have? Write the number sentence and solve the problem on the line below.

Lesson 121

1. Circle the unit Jim should use to measure the length of his watchband.

   inch   pound   gallon   mile

2. Amber earned $4 baby-sitting. Later, she earned $5 baby-sitting. How much money in all did Amber earn baby-sitting?
   Amber earned $_____ baby-sitting.

3. 13 − 9 =

4. 18 + 1 =

5. 25 − 11 =

Lesson 122

1. 13 + 6 =

2. 9 + 10 =

3. 19 − 7 =

4. Look at the bar graph. How many hours did Lisa work on Monday and Tuesday?
   Lisa worked _____ hours on Monday and Tuesday.

5. Jen bought 10 oranges on Sunday and 3 oranges on Monday. Draw a picture in the box to show your answer. Then, fill in the blank.
   Jen bought a total of _____ oranges.

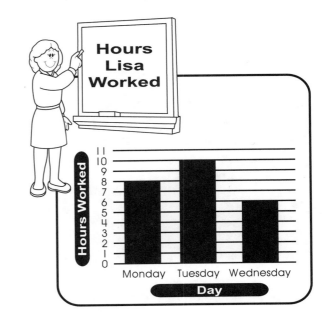

Hours Lisa Worked

Hours Worked

11 10 9 8 7 6 5 4 3 2 1 0

Monday   Tuesday   Wednesday

Day

Lesson 123

1. Tyrone caught 11 fish one day. The next day he caught 9 more fish. How many fish did Tyrone catch in all?

   Tyrone caught _____ fish.

2. How many fish long is the fishing rod?

   The fishing rod is _____ fish long.

3. $13 - 5 =$

4. $5 + 14 =$

5. $6 - 2 =$

Lesson 124

1. $22 - 11 =$

2. $5 + 35 =$

3. $16 - 9 =$

4. How many centimeters long is the dog's bone?

   The dog's bone is _____ centimeters long.

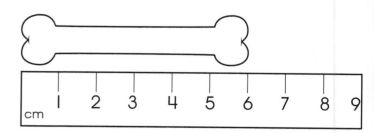

5. A gardener planted 7 trees in one row and 12 trees in another row. How many trees did he plant in all?

   The gardener planted _____ trees in all.

Lesson 125

1. It snowed 13 days during January and 15 days during the month of February. How many days did it snow during January and February?

    It snowed _____ days during January and February.

2. 35 + 30 =

3. 29 – 10 =

4. 13 + 6 =

5. Look at the picture graph. How many more students have brown eyes than blue eyes?

    _____ more students have brown eyes than blue eyes.

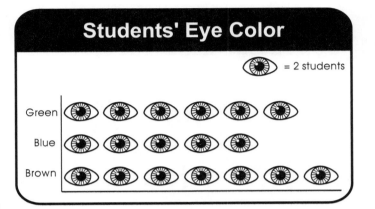

Students' Eye Color

= 2 students

Green
Blue
Brown

Lesson 126

1. How many inches long is the piece of yarn?

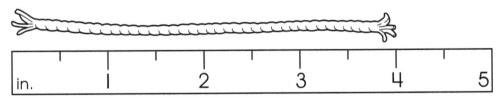

    The piece of yarn is _____ inches long.

2. Blake has 10 hats. She gives away 4 hats. How many hats does Blake have left?

    Blake has _____ hats left.

3. 29 – 9 =

4. 18 + 11 =

5. 8 + 12 =

Lesson 127

1. $5 + 15 =$

2. $14 - 10 =$

3. $14 + 3 =$

4. How many inches long is the rectangle? _____ inches long

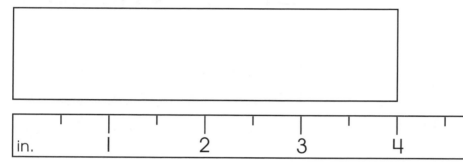

5. Owen packs 15 towels for the pool party. If 8 towels were used, how many towels were not used?

   _____ towels were not used.

Lesson 128

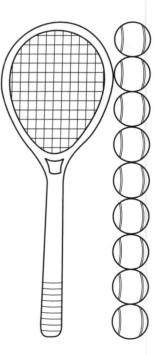

1. How many tennis balls tall is the picture of the tennis racket?

   The tennis racket is _____ tennis balls tall.

2. Anya types for 6 hours. Later, she types for 5 more hours. How many hours did Anya type in all?

   Anya typed for _____ hours.

3. $16 - 2 =$

4. $15 - 9 =$

5. $22 + 5 =$

Lesson 129

1. $45 + 10 =$

2. How many blocks tall is the baby?

   _____ blocks tall

3. $45 - 10 =$

4. $11 + 6 =$

5. A.J. has 10 cousins. If 4 of her cousins are older, how many of her cousins are younger?

   _____ of her cousins are younger.

Lesson 130

1. $9 - 4 =$

2. $14 + 12 =$

3. $17 - 6 =$

4. Jason worked on an art project for 14 days. Brian worked on the same art project for 11 days. How many more days did Jason work on the project than Brian?

   Jason worked _____ more days on the project.

5. Look at the bar graph. How many people have birthdays during February and April?

   _____ people have birthdays during February and April.

Number of Birthdays

Lesson 131

1. Fill in the blanks with numbers to complete the fact family for these numbers. 4, 3, and 7

_____ + _____ = _____   _____ + _____ = _____

_____ − _____ = _____   _____ − _____ = _____

2. Angela orders 8 sandwiches. If 5 sandwiches are turkey, how many of the sandwiches are not turkey?

_____ sandwiches are not turkey.

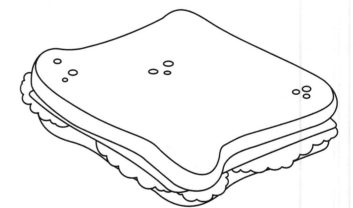

3. $14 + 5 =$

4. $14 − 7 =$

5. $2 + 9 =$

Lesson 132

1. Fill in the blank with <, >, or = to make the number sentence true.

33 _____ 17

2. There are 12 players on a school team. If 3 players did not attend a game, how many players did attend the game?

_____ players did attend the game.

3. $3 + 8 =$

4. $10 − 7 =$

5. $12 + 5 =$

Lesson 133

1. Fill in the blank with <, >, or = to make the number sentence true.

   27 _____ 14

2. Laurel stamped 10 letters. Later, she stamped 12 more letters. How many letters did Laurel stamp in all?

   Laurel stamped _____ letters in all.

3. $15 + 14 =$

4. $15 - 9 =$

5. $4 + 9 =$

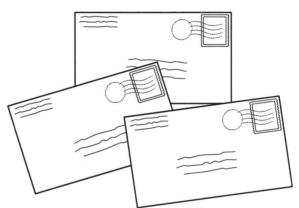

Lesson 134

1. $22 - 12 =$

2. $15 + 20 =$

3. $16 - 5 =$

4. Spot chewed 6 bones in the morning and 9 bones in the afternoon. How many bones did Spot chew in all?

   Spot chewed _____ bones in all.

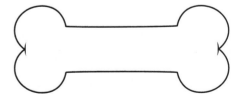

5. Fill in the blank with <, >, or = to make the number sentence true.

   55 _____ 55

Name _____

Lesson 135

1. Fill in the blanks with numbers to complete the fact family for these numbers. 11, 3, and 8

    _____ + _____ = _____   _____ + _____ = _____

    _____ − _____ = _____   _____ − _____ = _____

2. Bill sells 15 newspapers one day. He sells 6 newspapers the next day. How many more newspapers did Bill sell on the first day?

    Bill sold _____ more newspapers on the first day.

3. 19 − 9 =

4. 10 + 7 =

5. 5 − 5 =

Lesson 136

1. Draw the next shape in the pattern.

          _____

2. Dylan has art class 3 days a week. Each art class lasts for 2 hours. How many hours a week does Dylan spend in art class?

    Dylan spends _____ hours a week in art class.

3. 6 + 6 =

4. 12 + 7 =

5. 19 − 3 =

Lesson 137

1. Amed has 3 shelves in his room. Each shelf has 3 toys on it. How many toys are on all 3 shelves combined?

   There are _____ toys on all three shelves combined.

2. $11 - 0 =$

3. $17 - 6 =$

4. $17 + 11 =$

5. Fill in the blank to complete the pattern.

   5, 5, 1, 6, 6, 1, 7, 7, 1, _____, 8, 1

Lesson 138

1. $4 + 8 =$

2. $9 - 1 =$

3. $7 + 8 =$

4. Lynette fills up 4 bags with blankets. She puts 2 blankets in each bag. Draw a picture in the box to show the total number of blankets Lynette has. Then, fill in the blank.

   Lynette has _____ blankets altogether.

5. Fill in the blank with a number to make the number sentence true.

   $7 +$ _____ $+ 2 = 12$

Lesson 139

1. Sachi received 17 phone calls last Wednesday. Last Thursday, she only received 5 phone calls. How many more phone calls did Sachi receive on Wednesday?

   Sachi received _____ more phone calls on Wednesday.

2. $4 + 14 =$

3. $9 - 6 =$

4. $22 + 15 =$

5. Fill in the blanks with numbers to complete the fact family for these numbers. 5, 2, and 7

   _____ + _____ = _____   _____ + _____ = _____

   _____ − _____ = _____   _____ − _____ = _____

Lesson 140

1. $18 - 5 =$

2. $48 + 51 =$

3. $16 - 13 =$

4. There are 4 camels in the desert. Each camel has 2 humps. How many humps do the camels have altogether?

   The camels have _____ humps altogether.

5. Fill in the blank with a letter to complete the pattern.

   A, C, E, G, _____, K, M

Lesson 141

1. 10 + 17 =

2. 14 − 9 =

3. 12 + 7 =

5. There were 16 friends at Evan's birthday party. If 13 friends ate cake, how many friends did not eat cake?

    _____ friends did not eat cake.

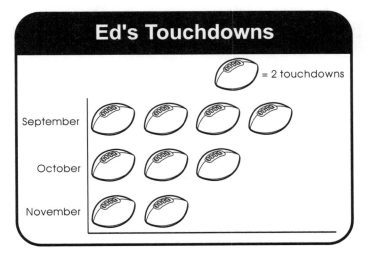

Ed's Touchdowns

= 2 touchdowns

September

October

November

4. Look at the picture graph. How many touchdowns did Ed score in September, October, and November altogether?

    Ed scored _____ touchdowns in September, October, and November altogether.

Lesson 142

1. 11 − 8 =

2. 10 + 65 =

3. 40 − 10 =

4. Look at the bar graph. How many kites were at the park on Saturday and Sunday?

    _____ kites were at the park on Saturday and Sunday.

5. Julie shared 6 flowers evenly with her friend. How many flowers did each girl get?

    Each girl got _____ flowers.

Kites at the Park

Number of Kites

18
17
16
15
14
13
12
11
10
9
8
7
6
5
4
3
2
1
0

Sat.   Sun.   Mon.

Day of the Week

Lesson 143

1. $3 + 17 =$

2. $50 - 20 =$

3. $50 + 45 =$

4. Look at the graph. How many days of sunshine were there in May and June?

    There were _____ days of sunshine in May and June.

5. There are 11 trees in Greg's yard. If 5 trees have flowers on them and the rest do not, how many of the trees do not have flowers?

    _____ of the trees do not have flowers.

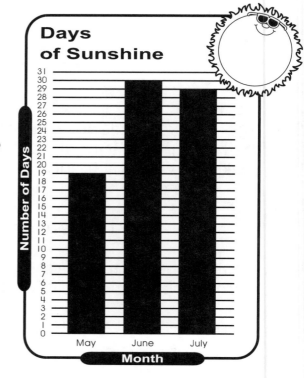

Days of Sunshine

Number of Days

31 30 29 28 27 26 25 24 23 22 21 20 19 18 17 16 15 14 13 12 11 10 9 8 7 6 5 4 3 2 1 0

May   June   July

Month

Lesson 144

1. Out of a class of 18 students, 7 students have curly hair. How many students do not have curly hair?

    _____ students do not have curly hair.

2. Look at the picture graph. How many tires needed repair on Tuesday and Thursday?

    _____ tires needed repair on Tuesday and Thursday.

3. $7 + 7 =$

4. $25 - 5 =$

5. $22 + 16 =$

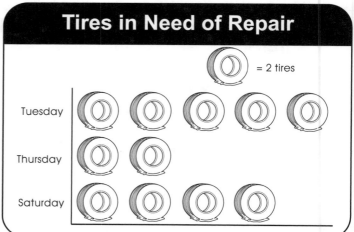

Tires in Need of Repair

= 2 tires

Tuesday

Thursday

Saturday

Lesson 145

1. Look at the bar graph. How many more points did Tara score in March than in January?

   Tara scored _____ more points in March than in January.

2. $16 - 4 =$

3. $4 + 24 =$

4. $32 + 5 =$

5. Sabena has 17 blue balloons and 3 red balloons. How many balloons does Sabena have in all?
   Write the number sentence and solve the problem on the line below.

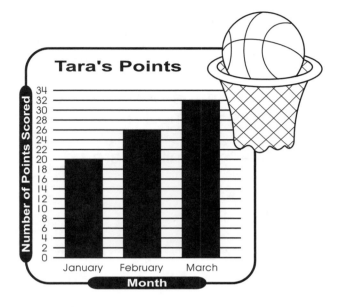

Tara's Points

Number of Points Scored

January   February   March

Month

Lesson 146

1. Skip has 13 music tapes. If 7 of the tapes are rock and roll and the rest are country and western, how many of the tapes are country and western?

   Skip has _____ country and western tapes.

2. Look at the bar graph. How many pairs of school shoes and dress shoes are in Allie's closet?

   There are _____ pairs of school shoes and dress shoes in Allie's closet.

3. $14 + 5 =$

4. $25 - 4 =$

5. $22 + 3 =$

Pairs of Shoes in Allie's Closet

Number

School   Dress   Sport

Shoe Type

Lesson 147

1. Andrew hit 2 home runs on Saturday and 5 home runs on Sunday. How many more home runs did he hit on Sunday?
    Andrew hit _____ more home runs on Sunday.

2. Look at the bar graph. On which day were the most miles traveled?

    The most miles were traveled on _____ .

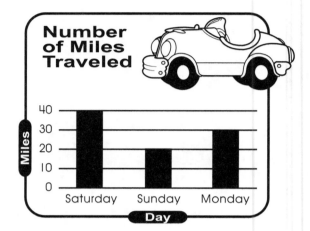

3. $12 + 13 =$

4. $28 - 6 =$

5. $16 + 3 =$

Lesson 148

1. Jeff mailed 10 letters one day and 6 letters the next. How many more letters did Jeff mail on the first day?

    Jeff mailed _____ more letters the first day.

2. Circle the picture that shows 3 groups of 5 stars.

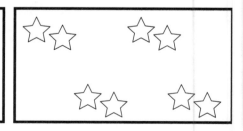

3. $13 - 8 =$

4. $6 + 14 =$

5. $19 - 1 =$

Lesson 149

1. Ellen bought 12 eggs at the grocery store. If 8 eggs broke on the way home from the store, how many eggs does Ellen have left?
    Ellen has _____ eggs left.

2. Circle the picture that shows 10 squares divided into 2 equal groups.

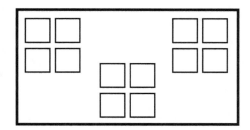 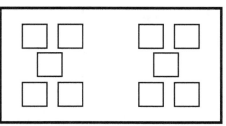 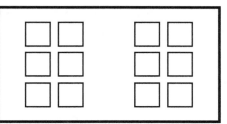

3. 12 + 3 =

4. 16 − 7 =

5. 10 + 11 =

Lesson 150

1. Mason sold 15 candy bars one day. He sold 9 candy bars the following day. How many candy bars did Mason sell in all?

    Mason sold _____ candy bars.

2. Circle the picture that shows 2 groups of 4 circles.

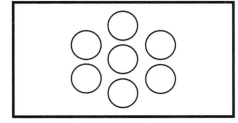 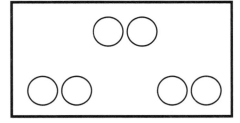 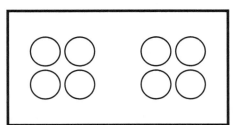

3. 15 − 9 =

4. 16 − 13 =

5. 12 + 14 =

Lesson 151

1. Miranda orders 17 scarves. If 12 scarves come in the mail Monday, how many more scarves still need to come?

    _____ more scarves still need to come.

2. What number do the Base Ten Blocks show?

    _____

3. $21 + 9 =$

4. $15 - 4 =$

5. $29 - 14 =$

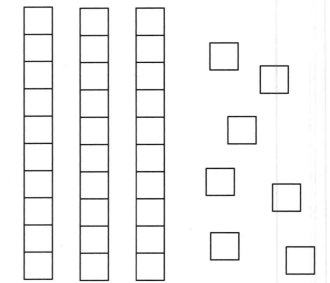

Lesson 152

1. Shawna has 21 baseball cards. She gives away 11 cards. How many cards does she have left?

    Shawna has _____ cards left.

2. $73 + 26 =$

3. $18 - 2 =$

4. $8 + 6 =$

5. Put the following numbers in order from least to greatest.
    76, 18, 54, 31

    _____, _____, _____, _____

Lesson 153

1. Selena hangs up 10 pictures one day. She hangs up 8 pictures the next day. How many pictures does she hang up in all?

   She hangs up _____ pictures in all.

2. $19 - 6 =$

3. $22 + 2 =$

4. $30 - 10 =$

5. What number do the Base Ten Blocks show?

   _____

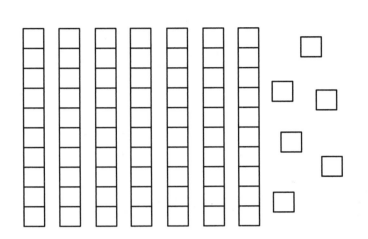

Lesson 154

1. $17 + 11 =$

2. $49 - 23 =$

3. $14 - 8 =$

4. Circle the shamrock that shows a correctly drawn line of symmetry.

5. Theresa orders 16 cupcakes for the party. If 9 cupcakes have candles on them, how many cupcakes do not have candles?

   _____ cupcakes do not have candles.

Lesson 155

1. $13 + 11 =$

2. $27 - 4 =$

3. $40 - 10 =$

4. Owen washed 18 towels. If 9 towels are blue, how many towels are not blue?

    _____ of the towels are not blue.

5. Draw one line of symmetry through the heart.

Lesson 156

1. Circle the shape that is the same as the shape in the box.

  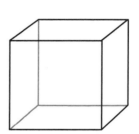 

2. Kamilla collects ladybugs. She collected 13 ladybugs in one jar and 13 more ladybugs in another jar. How many ladybugs did she collect in all?

    Kamilla collected _____ ladybugs in all.

3. $10 - 3 =$

4. $26 - 16 =$

5. $26 + 12 =$

Lesson 157

1. $21 - 1 =$

2. $12 + 12 =$

3. $19 - 11 =$

4. Garrett has 12 papers in his folder. If he gives 7 papers to his teacher, how many papers does he have left?
Garrett has _____ papers left.

5. Circle the shape that is the same as the shape in the box.

 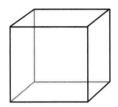  

Lesson 158

1. $80 - 10 =$

2. $25 + 11 =$

3. $7 + 9 =$

4. What number do the Base Ten Blocks show? _____

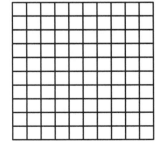 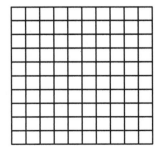 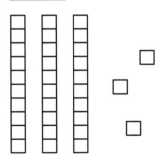

5. Mike drew 16 triangles. He colored 8 triangles orange and left the rest white. How many triangles did he leave white?
Mike left _____ triangles white.

Lesson 159

1. Adam bought 23 apples. If 11 apples are red and the rest are green, how many green apples did Adam buy?

    Adam bought _____ green apples.

2. 27 + 10 =

3. 3 – 3 =

4. 10 – 8 =

5. In the box, draw Base Ten Blocks to show the number 231.

Lesson 160

1. 24 + 10 =

2. 37 – 7 =

3. 12 – 9 =

4. Kathy bought 19 palm trees. She planted 8 palm trees in her front yard. How many palm trees does Kathy have left to plant in her backyard?

    Kathy has _____ palm trees left for her backyard.

5. Circle the star.

  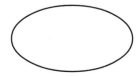

Name _____

Lesson 161

1. $15 - 5 =$

2. $24 - 11 =$

3. $26 + 3 =$

4. Porchia has 18 stickers. She wants to share them with her friend, Naomi. Draw a picture in the box to show how many stickers each girl will get.

   Each girl will get _____ stickers.

5. Fill in the blank with <, >, or = to make the number sentence true.

   14 _____ 41

Lesson 162

1. What is the total of the lengths of the sides of the triangle?

   _____ + _____ + _____ = _____ inches

2. Dana rode her bike 15 miles on Friday and 26 miles on Saturday. How many more miles did Dana ride her bike on Saturday?

   Dana rode her bike _____ more miles on Saturday.

3. $19 - 12 =$

4. $6 + 8 =$

5. $14 + 5 =$

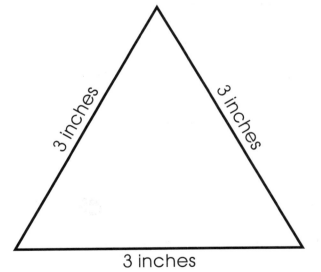

3 inches

Lesson 163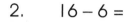

1. Philip picked 29 strawberries. Later, he ate 12 strawberries. How many strawberries does Philip have left?

   Philip has _____ strawberries left.

2. $16 - 6 =$

3. $22 + 7 =$

4. $60 - 30 =$

5. Fill in the blank with <, >, or = to make the number sentence true.

   31 _____ 13

Lesson 164

1. Fill in the blank with <, >, or = to make the number sentence true.

   2 _____ 12

2. Pedro collects comic books. If Pedro owns 6 comic books and his dad gives him 3 more comic books, how many comic books will Pedro own then?

   Pedro will own _____ comic books.

3. $9 + 9 =$

4. $12 - 7 =$

5. $21 + 8 =$

Lesson 165

1. Iesha made 30 sugar cookies. She decorated 20 sugar cookies. How many sugar cookies were not decorated?

   _____ cookies were not decorated.

2. $16 - 9 =$

3. $15 + 12 =$

4. $24 - 13 =$

5. What is the total of the lengths of the sides of the rectangle?

   _____ + _____ + _____ + _____ =

   _____ centimeters

4 centimeters

3 centimeters

3 centimeters

4 centimeters

Lesson 166

1. About how many buttons tall is the notepad?

   The notepad is about _____ buttons tall.

2. $10 + 50 =$

3. $50 - 10 =$

4. $17 - 14 =$

5. Katherine counted 17 horses in the barn. If 9 horses are eating, how many horses are not eating?

   _____ of the horses are not eating.

Lesson 167

1. What is the total of the lengths of the sides of the square?

   _____ + _____ + _____ + _____ = _____ inches

2 inches

2. $33 - 13 =$

3. $20 + 7 =$

4. $22 - 2 =$

5. Denise had 4 baskets with treats. There were 6 treats in each basket. Draw a picture in the box to show the total number of treats Denise had. Then, fill in the blank.
   Denise had _____ treats in all.

Lesson 168

1. Travis is reading a book that is 100 pages long. He read 30 pages last Tuesday. How many more pages does Travis have left to read?

   Travis has _____ more pages left to read.

2. $34 + 14 =$

3. $36 - 6 =$

4. $28 + 10 =$

5. How many nails long is the hammer?

   The hammer is _____ nails long.

Lesson 169

1. Molly has 3 bags full of books. Each bag holds 3 books. Draw a picture in the box to show the total number of books Molly has. Then, fill in the blank.

   Molly has _____ books.

2. $27 - 4 =$

3. $35 - 10 =$

4. $36 + 11 =$

5. Fill in the blank with <, >, or = to make the number sentence true.
   17 _____ 17

Lesson 170

1. At the pet store, 2 dogs had puppies. Each dog had 7 puppies. Draw a picture in the box to show the number of puppies the dogs have altogether. Then, fill in the blank.

   The dogs have _____ puppies altogether.

2. $13 - 9 =$

3. $13 + 6 =$

4. $44 + 44 =$

5. Fill in the blank with + or – to make the number sentence true.
   18 _____ 6 = 12

Lesson 171

1. A roll of film contains 24 pictures. If 4 pictures have been taken, how many pictures have not been taken?
   _____ pictures have not been taken.

2. $8 + 8 =$

3. $19 - 6 =$

4. $27 - 11 =$

5. Circle the picture that shows 3 groups of 9 leaves.

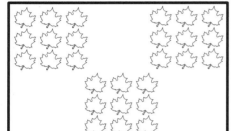 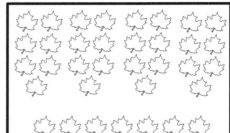 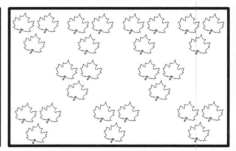

Lesson 172

1. If 5 children are in line and each child has 2 tickets, how many tickets do the children have altogether? (Hint: Draw a picture.)
   The children have _____ tickets altogether.

2. $40 - 20 =$

3. $38 - 10 =$

4. $32 + 6 =$

5. Circle the picture that shows 12 bells divided into 3 equal groups.

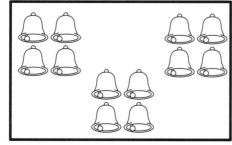  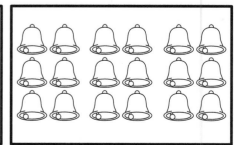

Name _____

Lesson 173

1. Circle the picture that shows 3 groups of 3 circles.

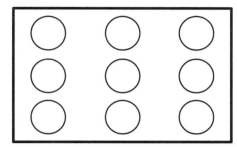 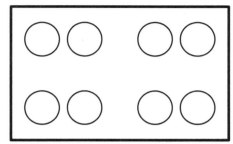 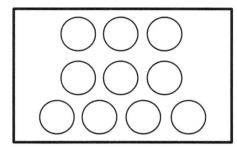

2. 51 + 23 =

3. 69 – 54 =

4. 38 – 7 =

5. There are 4 nests in a tree. Each nest has 4 eggs. How many eggs are there in all? (Hint: Draw a picture.)
   There are _____ eggs in all.

Lesson 174

1. 30 – 20 =

2. 29 + 1 =

3. 75 + 13 =

4. Zach mowed 16 lawns on Saturday and 12 lawns on Monday. How many lawns did Zach mow in all?
   Zach mowed a total of _____ lawns.

5. Circle the picture that shows 15 lightbulbs divided into 5 equal groups.

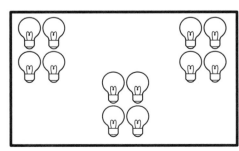 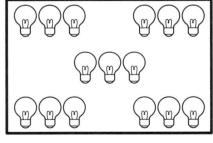 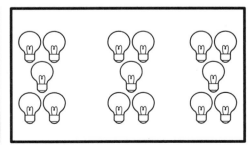

Lesson 175

1. T.J. has 2 shelves in his room. He puts 4 books on each shelf. How many books are on the shelves in all? (Hint: Draw a picture.)

   There are _____ books in all.

2. $16 - 5 =$

3. $20 + 34 =$

4. $34 - 20 =$

5. Look at the bar graph. How many more people visited the pool on Saturday than on Sunday?

   _____ more people visited the pool on Saturday than on Sunday.

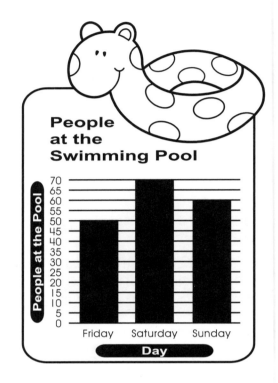

Lesson 176

1. At the circus, there are 7 monkeys, 9 elephants, and 2 camels. How many more elephants than monkeys are there?
   There are _____ more elephants than monkeys.

2. Look at the picture graph. How many more people visited the pool on Tuesday than on Wednesday?
   _____ more people visited the pool on Tuesday than on Wednesday.

3. $72 - 10 =$

4. $14 + 15 =$

5. $18 - 6 =$

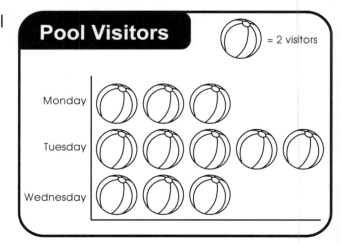

Lesson 177

1. Bradley has 27 rocks in his collection. If he took 11 rocks to show-and-tell, how many rocks did Bradley leave at home?
   Bradley left _____ rocks at home.

2. $18 - 9 =$

3. $16 - 1 =$

4. $20 + 44 =$

5. Circle the picture that shows 10 kites divided into 5 equal groups.

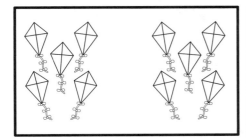 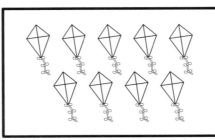 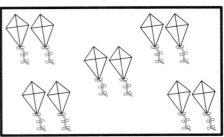

Lesson 178

1. Circle the picture that shows 4 groups of 3 cars.

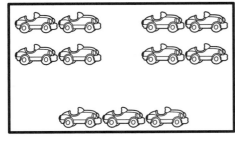 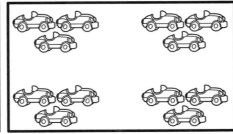 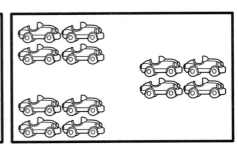

2. $11 - 3 =$

3. $27 + 20 =$

4. $15 - 8 =$

5. There are 17 cars at a stoplight. If 6 cars have their lights on, how many cars do not have their lights on?
   _____ cars do not have their lights on.

 Daily Math Warm-Ups Grade 1

Name _____

Lesson 179

1. Look at the bar graph. How many hot dogs and corn dogs were sold at the game?

   _____ hot dogs and corn dogs were sold at the game.

2. Brianna and her dad bought 2 hot dogs, 3 bags of popcorn, and 2 ice cream cones. How many items did they buy in all?
   They bought _____ items in all.

3. $15 + 14 =$

4. $26 - 12 =$

5. $24 + 24 =$

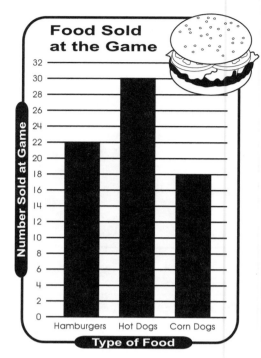

Food Sold at the Game

Number Sold at Game

Type of Food: Hamburgers, Hot Dogs, Corn Dogs

Lesson 180

1. $21 + 22 =$

2. $15 - 9 =$

3. $71 + 17 =$

4. Norma found 32 erasers at the bottom of her school box. She gave 1 eraser to each of the 20 students in her class. How many erasers does Norma have left?
   Norma has _____ erasers left.

5. Circle the picture that shows 4 groups of 2 music notes.

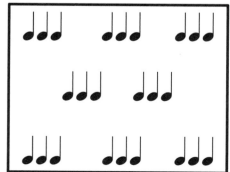
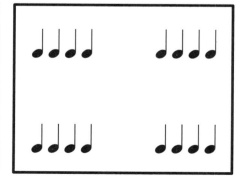
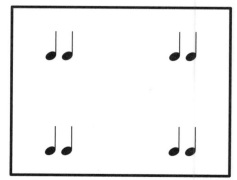

Answer Key: Lessons 1–20

Lesson 1
1. 9
2. 8
3. 4
4. 12
5. 9

Lesson 2
1. 1, 2, 5, 8
2. 2
3. 10
4. 12
5. 4

Lesson 3
1. 3
2. 18
3. 10
4. 10
5. $3 + 1 = 4$

Lesson 4
1. $5 + 2 = 7$
2. 2
3. 10
4. 10
5. My Classmates' Pets

Lesson 5
1. 2
2. 4
3. 15
4. 4
5. 12, 13, 14, 15, 16

Lesson 6
1. 32
2. 11
3. 20
4. 14
5. 10

Lesson 7
1. 7
2. 5
3. 0, 9, 10, 17
4. 10
5. 3 balloons drawn

Lesson 8
1. 16
2. 11
3. 14
4. $11 + 5 = 16$
5. 9

Lesson 9
1.
= 1 call

2. 15
3. 14
4. 82
5. $6 + 3 = 9$

Lesson 10
1. $7 + 3 = 10$
2. 15
3. 17
4. 1
5. 18

Lesson 11
1. 4 circled
2. cube drawn
3. 12 flowers drawn
4. 19
5. 5

Lesson 12
1. Colors: red, blue, orange; Numbers: six, four, three, zero
2. 17
3. 5
4. 18
5. 10

Lesson 13
1. 6
2. 14
3. 57
4. +
5. 3

Lesson 14
1. 10
2. 19
3. 7
4. 13
5. 5 cookies each drawn

Lesson 15
1. 2
2. 12
3. $9 - 3 = 6$ apples drawn
4. 20
5. 10

Lesson 16
1. 2; 3
2. 11
3. 7
4. 9
5. subtract; subtract circled

Lesson 17
1. 12
2. D
3. $10 - 7 = 3$ balls drawn; 3
4. 6
5. 7

Lesson 18
1. $5 - 2 = 3$
2. 9
3. 8
4. 5
5. 19

Lesson 19
1. 10
2. rectangle
3. 7
4. 7
5. 10

Lesson 20
1. 27
2. 15
3. 2
4. 5
5. 8

Answer Key: Lessons 21–41

Lesson 21
1. 2
2. 17
3. orange
4. 11
5. 8

Lesson 22
1. 2 scoops
2. 12
3. 10
4. 3
5. 5

Lesson 23
1. 1
2. 8
3. <
4. 2
5. 15

Lesson 24
1. pink
2. 1
3. <
4. 4
5. 11

Lesson 25
1. 4
2. 16
3. pen
4. 14
5. 17

Lesson 26
1. 3
2. 2
3. 5
4. 18
5. 9

Lesson 27
1. hats
2. 9
3. =
4. 6
5. 3

Lesson 28
1. 5
2. 1
3. >
4. 6
5. 9

Lesson 29
1. 2
2. 8
3. 4
4. 8
5. 8

Lesson 30
1. dog
2. 13
3. 3
4. 5
5. 0

Lesson 31
1.
2. 4
3. 40
4. 4
5. 7

Lesson 32
1. 14
2.
3. 70
4.
5. 3

Lesson 33
1.
2. 15
3. 9
4. 60
5. 3

Lesson 34
1. triangle; 3 sides; 3 corners
2. 16
3. 20
4. 9
5. 16

Lesson 35
1. 7
2. circle
3. 16
4. 8
5. 25

Lesson 36
1. 2 + 2 + 2 = 6
2. 20
3. 7
4. 20
5. 5

Lesson 37
1.
2. 4
3. 14
4. 7
5. 100

Lesson 38
1. 10
2. 100
3. triangle circled
4. 20
5.

Lesson 39
1. 19
2. 20
3. rectangle
4. 26
5. 17

Lesson 40
1. 5
2. 19
3. 12
4. 9
5. 10

Lesson 41
1. 20
2. 30
3. 30
4. Sunday
5. 18

Answer Key: Lessons 42–62

Lesson 42
1. 16
2. 10
3. 14
4. 19
5. 15

Lesson 43
1. 4
2. 11
3. 3
4. 6
5. 7

Lesson 44
1. 20
2. 10
3. 40
4. 34
5. brown

Lesson 45
1. 6
2. 13
3. 1
4. 30
5. 60

Lesson 46
1. 4 – 2 = 2 shirts drawn; 2
2. >
3. <
4. <
5. 50

Lesson 47
1. 10
2. 10
3. 9
4. 0
5. 6 o'clock

Lesson 48
1. 8
2. group of 15 circled
3. 110
4. 7
5. 20

Lesson 49
1. 5
2. 21
3. 18
4. 8
5. 20

Lesson 50
1. heart
2. 2
3. 6
4. 4
5. 11

Lesson 51
1. 11
2. 6
3. 17
4. 6
5. 100

Lesson 52
1.
2. 8
3. 14
4. 6
5. 4 o'clock

Lesson 53
1. 16
2. 7 o'clock
3. 12
4. 20
5. 70

Lesson 54
1. 18
2. 19
3. 75
4. 21
5. ; 4

Lesson 55
1. 15
2. 80
3. 60
4. 30
5. circle drawn

Lesson 56
1. 14
2. 19
3. 19
4. 15
5. square circled

Lesson 57
1. 8
2. 32
3. 15
4. 20
5. 2

Lesson 58
1. 9
2. 14
3. 18
4. 19
5. 5

Lesson 59
1. 15
2. 22
3. 18
4. 24
5. square circled

Lesson 60
1. 11
2. 1
3. 20
4. 21
5.

Lesson 61
1. 2
2. 4
3. 20
4. 17
5. Answers will vary

Lesson 62
1. 13
2. 29
3. 8
4. 18
5. 2

Answer Key: Lessons 63–84

Lesson 63
1. 2
2. 20
3. 20
4. 20
5. 16

Lesson 64
1. Ellie
2. 22
3. 4
4. 45
5. flower drawn

Lesson 65
1. 3
2. 20
3. 9
4. 17
5. 24

Lesson 66
1. oval drawn
2. 13
3. 5
4. 19
5. 3

Lesson 67
1. Class 3
2. 10
3. 28
4. 17
5. 25

Lesson 68
1. 26
2. 11
3. 12
4. 50
5. 2

Lesson 69
1. 4
2. 8
3. 8
4. 5
5. 8

Lesson 70
1. 2
2. 20
3. 21
4. 5
5. 100

Lesson 71
1. 28
2. 34
3. 20
4. 6
5. 20

Lesson 72
1. 19
2. 11
3. 34
4. 6
5. 4

Lesson 73
1. 5
2. 95
3. 21
4. 20
5. 7

Lesson 74
1. 8
2. 2
3. 4
4. 19
5. 85

Lesson 75
1. 11
2. 90
3. 0
4. 17
5. 18

Lesson 76
1. 2
2. 14
3. 13
4. 50
5. 5

Lesson 77
1. circle drawn
2. 4
3. 70
4. 13
5. 6

Lesson 78
1. $2 + 7 = 9$;
   $7 + 2 = 9$;
   $9 - 2 = 7$;
   $9 - 7 = 2$
2. 7
3. 29
4. 13
5. 8

Lesson 79
1. 20
2. 28
3. 13
4. 13
5. 9

Lesson 80
1. 40
2. 10
3. 17
4. 18, 20
5. 50

Lesson 81
1. 16
2. 54
3. 36
4. 20
5. 7

Lesson 82
1. 20
2. 30
3. 13
4. 2
5. 10

Lesson 83
1. 9
2. 65
3. 90
4. 90
5. 5

Lesson 84
1. 20
2. 58
3. 8
4. 81
5. $5 + 8 = 13$;
   $13 - 8 = 5$;
   $13 - 5 = 8$

Answer Key: Lessons 85–105

Lesson 85
1. 34
2. 33
3. 50
4. 10
5. 7

Lesson 86
1. 5 + 3 = 8;
   3 + 5 = 8;
   8 − 5 = 3
2. 9
3. 40
4. 8
5. 38

Lesson 87
1. 19
2. 9
3. 3
4. 13
5. 7 + 11 = 18

Lesson 88
1. 11
2. 0
3. 12
4. 15
5. 70

Lesson 89
1. 8
2. 10
3. 58
4. 50
5. 90

Lesson 90
1. 6
2. 10
3. 71
4. 33
5. 3 + 6 = 9;
   6 + 3 = 9;
   9 − 6 = 3;
   9 − 3 = 6

Lesson 91
1. 3
2. 8
3. 25
4. 43
5. 60

Lesson 92
1. 15
2. 3
3. 29
4. 10 circled
5. 9

Lesson 93
1. 9
2. 9
3. 18
4. 25
5. 10, 15, 25, 51

Lesson 94
1.

2. 15
3. 25
4. 2
5. 5

Lesson 95
1. 40
2. 22
3. 37
4. 18
5.

Lesson 96
1. 30
2. 4
3. 3
4. 20
5. 7

Lesson 97
1. 9
2. 70
3. 5
4. 51
5. 4

Lesson 98
1. 34
2. 15
3.

4. 7
5. 30

Lesson 99
1. 62
2. 82
3. 15
4. 11
5. 16 − 9 = 7

Lesson 100
1. 5
2. 9
3. 6
4. 60
5. 8

Lesson 101
1. 11
2. 12
3. 40
4. 9
5. >

Lesson 102
1. >
2. 10
3. 16
4. 17
5. 8

Lesson 103
1. 11
2. 23
3. 43
4. 44
5. >

Lesson 104
1. 4
2. 27
3. 19
4. 90
5. 7

Lesson 105
1. 12
2. 21
3. 14
4. 6
5. 9

Answer Key: Lessons 106–126

Lesson 106
1. 5
2. 2
3. 19
4. 13
5. 10

Lesson 107
1. 0
2. 60
3. 14
4. 5
5. <

Lesson 108
1. 10
2. 80
3. 5
4. 9
5. +

Lesson 109
1. 8
2. 8
3. 8
4. 17
5. 10

Lesson 110
1. 2
2. 30
3. 10
4. 12
5. 7

Lesson 111
1. 4
2. 8
3. 21
4. 11
5.

Lesson 112
1. 4
2.
3. 20
4. 6
5. 8

Lesson 113
1. 11
2.
3. 30
4. 65
5. 20

Lesson 114
1. 9
2. 25
3. 9
4. 10
5.

Lesson 115
1. 22
2. 6
3. 7
4. 19
5. 14

Lesson 116
1. 13
2. 29
3. 2
4. 16
5.

Lesson 117
1. 6
2. 20
3. 19
4. 7
5. 23

Lesson 118
1. 6
2. 5
3. 5
4. 16
5.

Lesson 119
1.
2. 23
3. 7
4. 16
5. 90

Lesson 120
1. 22
2. 1
3. 19
4. 11
5. 13 + 12 = 25

Lesson 121
1. inch
2. $9
3. 4
4. 19
5. 14

Lesson 122
1. 19
2. 19
3. 12
4. 18
5. 10 + 3 = 13 oranges drawn; 13

Lesson 123
1. 20
2. 5
3. 8
4. 19
5. 4

Lesson 124
1. 11
2. 40
3. 7
4. 6
5. 19

Lesson 125
1. 28
2. 65
3. 19
4. 19
5. 4

Lesson 126
1. 4
2. 6
3. 20
4. 29
5. 20

Answer Key: Lessons 127–147

Lesson 127
1. 20
2. 4
3. 17
4. 4
5. 7

Lesson 128
1. 9
2. 11
3. 14
4. 6
5. 27

Lesson 129
1. 55
2. 9
3. 35
4. 17
5. 6

Lesson 130
1. 5
2. 26
3. 11
4. 3
5. 35

Lesson 131
1. 4 + 3 = 7;
   3 + 4 = 7;
   7 − 4 = 3;
   7 − 3 = 4
2. 3
3. 19
4. 7
5. 11

Lesson 132
1. >
2. 9
3. 11
4. 3
5. 17

Lesson 133
1. >
2. 22
3. 29
4. 6
5. 13

Lesson 134
1. 10
2. 35
3. 11
4. 15
5. =

Lesson 135
1. 3 + 8 = 11;
   8 + 3 = 11;
   11 − 8 = 3;
   11 − 3 = 8
2. 9
3. 10
4. 17
5. 0

Lesson 136
1. circle drawn
2. 6
3. 12
4. 19
5. 16

Lesson 137
1. 9
2. 11
3. 11
4. 28
5. 8

Lesson 138
1. 12
2. 8
3. 15
4. 4 x 2 = 8
   blankets
   drawn; 8
5. 3

Lesson 139
1. 12
2. 18
3. 3
4. 37
5. 5 + 2 = 7;
   2 + 5 = 7;
   7 − 2 = 5;
   7 − 5 = 2

Lesson 140
1. 13
2. 99
3. 3
4. 8
5. I

Lesson 141
1. 27
2. 5
3. 19
4. 3
5. 18

Lesson 142
1. 3
2. 75
3. 30
4. 28
5. 3

Lesson 143
1. 20
2. 30
3. 95
4. 49
5. 6

Lesson 144
1. 11
2. 14
3. 14
4. 20
5. 38

Lesson 145
1. 12
2. 12
3. 28
4. 37
5. 17 + 3 = 20

Lesson 146
1. 6
2. 9
3. 19
4. 21
5. 25

Lesson 147
1. 3
2. Saturday
3. 25
4. 22
5. 19

Answer Key: Lessons 148–167

Lesson 148
1. 4
2.
3. 5
4. 20
5. 18

Lesson 149
1. 4
2.
3. 15
4. 9
5. 21

Lesson 150
1. 24
2.
3. 6
4. 3
5. 26

Lesson 151
1. 5
2. 37
3. 30
4. 11
5. 15

Lesson 152
1. 10
2. 99
3. 16
4. 14
5. 18, 31, 54, 76

Lesson 153
1. 18
2. 13
3. 24
4. 20
5. 76

Lesson 154
1. 28
2. 26
3. 6
4.
5. 7

Lesson 155
1. 24
2. 23
3. 30
4. 9
5.

Lesson 156
1. cube circled
2. 26
3. 7
4. 10
5. 38

Lesson 157
1. 20
2. 24
3. 8
4. 5
5. cone circled

Lesson 158
1. 70
2. 36
3. 16
4. 233
5. 8

Lesson 159
1. 12
2. 37
3. 0
4. 2
5.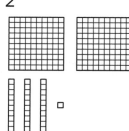

Lesson 160
1. 34
2. 30
3. 3
4. 11
5. star circled

Lesson 161
1. 10
2. 13
3. 29
4. 9 stickers drawn in each box; 9
5. <

Lesson 162
1. 3 + 3 + 3 = 9
2. 11
3. 7
4. 14
5. 19

Lesson 163
1. 17
2. 10
3. 29
4. 30
5. >

Lesson 164
1. <
2. 9
3. 18
4. 5
5. 29

Lesson 165
1. 10
2. 7
3. 27
4. 11
5. 4 + 4 + 3 + 3 = 14

Lesson 166
1. 7
2. 60
3. 40
4. 3
5. 8

Lesson 167
1. 2 + 2 + 2 + 2 = 8
2. 20
3. 27
4. 20
5. 4 x 6 = 24 treats drawn; 24

Answer Key: Lessons 168–180

Lesson 168
1. 70
2. 48
3. 30
4. 38
5. 8

Lesson 169
1. 3 x 3 = 9 books drawn; 9
2. 23
3. 25
4. 47
5. =

Lesson 170
1. 2 x 7 = 14 puppies drawn; 14
2. 4
3. 19
4. 88
5. −

Lesson 171
1. 20
2. 16
3. 7
4. 16
5.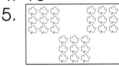

Lesson 172
1. 10
2. 20
3. 28
4. 38
5.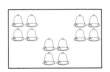

Lesson 173
1.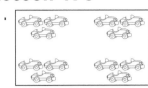
2. 74
3. 15
4. 31
5. 16

Lesson 174
1. 10
2. 30
3. 88
4. 28
5.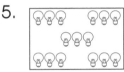

Lesson 175
1. 8
2. 11
3. 54
4. 14
5. 10

Lesson 176
1. 2
2. 4
3. 62
4. 29
5. 12

Lesson 177
1. 16
2. 9
3. 15
4. 64
5.

Lesson 178
1. [image of cars]
2. 8
3. 47
4. 7
5. 11

Lesson 179
1. 48
2. 7
3. 29
4. 14
5. 48

Lesson 180
1. 43
2. 6
3. 88
4. 12
5. [image of musical notes]

Assessment 1 (Lessons 1–10)

Name _____

1. 3 + 4 =

A. 7
B. 5
C. 1
D. 6

2. Look at the bar graph. What is the most popular color?

A. Green
B. Blue
C. Yellow
D. Red

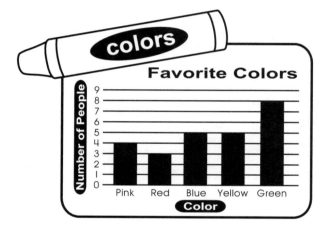

3. 7 + 4 =

A. 11
B. 12
C. 3
D. 4

4. Put the following numbers in order from least to greatest.
12, 5, 9, 15

A. 15, 12, 9, 5
B. 5, 9, 15, 12
C. 5, 9, 12, 15
D. 9, 12, 15, 5

5. 6 + 7 =

A. 13
B. 14
C. 18
D. 11

6. Which number is greatest?

A. 19
B. 30
C. 29
D. 33

7. There are 10 students in Ellen's class and 3 students like reading best. How many students do not like reading best?

A. 7
B. 3
C. 10
D. 9

8. Look at the picture graph. How many people ordered grilled cheese sandwiches at lunch?

A. 3
B. 4
C. 7
D. 8

☐ = 1 person

Lunch Orders

Hamburgers

Hot Dogs

Grilled Cheese

Turkey

Assessment 2 (Lessons 11–20)

Name _____

1. Which number will complete the pattern?
   3, 5, 7, _____, 11, 13

   A. 4
   B. 6
   C. 8
   D. 9

2. 8 – 7 =

   A.　1
   B.　2
   C.　14
   D.　15

3. Which sign should you use in an addition number sentence?

   A. x
   B. –
   C. +
   D. &

4. What number do the Base Ten Blocks show?

   A.　10
   B.　46
   C.　406
   D.　64

   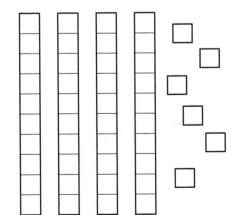

5. In the number 19, what number is in the tens place?

   A.　0
   B.　1
   C.　9
   D.　19

6. 7 + 9 =

   A.　11
   B.　15
   C.　2
   D.　16

7. 10 + 3 =

   A.　7
   B.　13
   C.　15
   D.　18

8. Look at the picture. The circle is divided into how many equal parts?

   A. 4

   B. 3

   C. 2

   D. 1

Assessment 3 (Lessons 21–30)

Name _____

1. 3 + 2 =

A. 15
B. 17
C. 8
D. 5

2. Which number should go in the blank to make the number sentence true?

6 + 3 + _____ = 15

A. 6
B. 3
C. 8
D. 15

3. What even number is greater than 11 but less than 13?

A. 14
B. 10
C. 12
D. 15

4. Look at the picture. If Rico reaches into the bag without looking, what shape is he most likely to pull out?

A. square
B. triangle
C. circle
D. rectangle

5. 6 – 5 =

A. 11
B. 0
C. 1
D. 2

6. Which sign will make the number sentence true?

11 _____ 1

A. =
B. <
C. >

7. Which number is greatest?

9, 18, 21, 5

A. 9
B. 18
C. 21
D. 5

8. Look at the spinner. What number is Betsy most likely to spin?

A. 2
B. 3
C. 7
D. 11

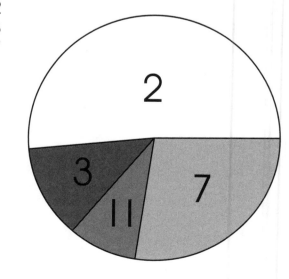

Assessment 4 (Lessons 31–40)

Name _____

1. 20 + 8 =

A. 12
B. 25
C. 28
D. 208

2. 20 + 10 =

A. 30
B. 21
C. 40
D. 3

3. What time is shown on the clock?

A. 6 o'clock
B. 8 o'clock
C. 5 o'clock
D. 12 o'clock

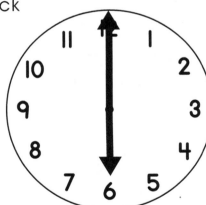

4. Henry walked 2 miles to school in the morning. After school, he walked 2 miles home. How many miles did Henry walk in all?

A. 2
B. 3
C. 4
D. 5

5. 9 – 9 =

A. 16
B. 1
C. 0
D. 18

6. Which shape has more than 4 sides?

A.
B.
C.
D.

7. Which letter shows a line of symmetry?

A. A
B. B
C. C
D. D

8. How many sides does this shape have?

A. 3
B. 4
C. 5
D. 2

Name _____

1. Estimate. Circle the best estimate for the answer to the problem.
   $31 + 29 =$

   A. 50
   B. 60
   C. 30
   D. 40

2. $10 - 5 =$

   A. 4
   B. 5
   C. 8
   D. 15

3. Which number will make this number sentence true?
   $14 - \underline{\quad} = 10$

   A. 4
   B. 7
   C. 24
   D. 0

4. Norma Kay has 15 cats. If 9 cats have stripes, how many cats do not have stripes?

   A. 8
   B. 6
   C. 11
   D. 15

5. Which number will make this number sentence true?
   $6 + \underline{\quad} + 3 = 18$

   A. 4
   B. 8
   C. 7
   D. 9

6. $50 + 10 =$

   A. 70
   B. 60
   C. 40
   D. 50

7. Which sign will make the number sentence true?
   $21 \underline{\quad} 12$

   A. $=$
   B. $<$
   C. $>$

8. Which group is the greatest?

   A.    B.

   C.    D.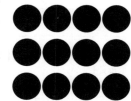

Assessment 6 (Lessons 51–60)

Name _____

1. 16 – 10 =

A. 21
B. 19
C. 10
D. 6

5. 30 + 10 =

A. 30
B. 40
C. 310
D. 20

2. There are 8 cats and 5 kittens on the farm. How many cats and kittens are there in all?

A. 8
B. 10
C. 18
D. 13

6. Ariel bought 16 cookies. She ate 3 cookies. How many cookies does she have left?

A. 13
B. 23
C. 10
D. 8

3. Paul studied for 2 hours. Later, he studied for 4 hours. How many hours did Paul study in all?

A. 2
B. 4
C. 6
D. 8

7. There are 20 students in music class and 10 students in art class. How many students in both classes combined?

A. 35
B. 25
C. 30
D. 15

4. How many hands high is the horse?

A. 7
B. 5
C. 3
D. 6

8. Look at the clock below. What time is shown on the clock?

A. 1:00
B. 12:00
C. 4:00
D. 2:00

1. 15 + 3 =

   A. 15
   B. 18
   C. 8
   D. 7

2. 12 – 7 =

   A. 4
   B. 5
   C. 18
   D. 19

3. 80 – 40 =

   A. 20
   B. 35
   C. 40
   D. 50

Use the picture graph to answer questions 4 through 8.

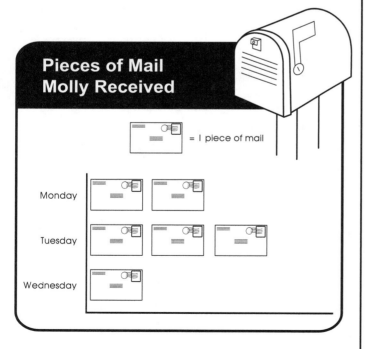

4. Each envelope = _____ piece of mail.

   A. 5
   B. 3
   C. 2
   D. 1

5. How many pieces of mail did Molly receive on Wednesday?

   A. 4
   B. 1
   C. 2
   D. 6

6. How many more pieces of mail did Molly receive on Monday than on Wednesday?

   A. 2
   B. 3
   C. 5
   D. 1

7. How many pieces of mail did Molly receive on Tuesday and Wednesday altogether?

   A. 4
   B. 7
   C. 6
   D. 2

8. On which day did Molly receive 3 pieces of mail?

   A. Monday
   B. Tuesday
   C. Wednesday
   D. Thursday

Assessment 8 (Lessons 71–80)

Name _____

Use the bar graph to answer questions 1 and 2.

Sidewalks Shoveled by Paul

1. How many more sidewalks did Paul shovel on Friday than on Saturday?

   A. 16
   B. 5
   C. 6
   D. 9

2. How many more sidewalks did Paul shovel on Sunday than on Saturday?

   A. 5
   B. 11
   C. 7
   D. 3

3. 18 + 10 =

   A. 8
   B. 22
   C. 28
   D. 32

4. Complete the pattern.
   27, 24, 21, 18, _____, 12

   A. 12
   B. 15
   C. 18
   D. 20

5. Complete the pattern.
   7, 14, _____, 28, 35, 42

   A. 18
   B. 15
   C. 20
   D. 21

6. 17 − 5 =

   A. 12
   B. 10
   C. 22
   D. 25

7. 18 − 9 =

   A. 10
   B. 9
   C. 7
   D. 27

8. There are 31 days in May. Susan will be out of town 10 days in May. How many days will Susan be home in May?

   A. 48
   B. 21
   C. 13
   D. 14

Assessment 9 (Lessons 81–90)

Name _____

Use the graph to answer 1, 2, and 3.

Movies Janie Went to See

= 1 movie

June
July
August

1. How many times total did Janie go to the movies in June, July, and August?

   A.   9
   B.   8
   C.   6
   D.   4

2. Each kernel = _____ movie.

   A.   2
   B.   4
   C.   3
   D.   1

3. In which month did Janie see the most movies?

   A.   May
   B.   June
   C.   July
   D.   August

4.   60 + 10 =

   A.   75
   B.   70
   C.   50
   D.   45

5. If 10 first graders like chocolate ice cream and 20 first graders like vanilla ice cream, how many more first graders like vanilla ice cream than chocolate ice cream?

   A.   8
   B.   7
   C.   10
   D.   30

6. Circle the answer that shows number sentences that belong to the same fact family as 8 + 4 = 12.

   A. $4 + 4 = 8$; $12 - 4 = 8$
   B. $12 - 8 = 4$; $4 + 8 = 12$
   C. $12 + 4 = 16$; $16 - 12 = 4$
   D. $12 + 4 = 16$; $14 + 12 = 26$

7. There are 18 glasses of ice water on a table. If 8 of the glasses have lemon in them, how many of the glasses do not have lemon in them?

   A.   4
   B.   5
   C.   10
   D.   26

8. The library has 23 chairs and 10 tables. How many more chairs than tables are in the library?

   A.   8
   B.   6
   C.   13
   D.   33

Assessment 10 (Lessons 91–100)   Name _____

1. A school has 20 round clocks and 9 square clocks. How many round and square clocks does the school have in all?

A. 29
B. 19
C. 15
D. 32

2. What time is shown on the clock?

A. 5:00
B. 12:00
C. 4:30
D. 6:30

3. Use the ruler to measure the key. How long is the key?

A. 3 centimeters
B. 3 inches
C. 2 inches
D. 3 feet

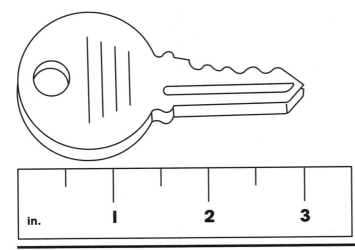

4. James drank 3 glasses of water before breakfast and 9 glasses of water after soccer practice. How many glasses of water did James drink in all?

A. 10
B. 12
C. 15
D. 25

5. 27 − 10 =

A. 16
B. 17
C. 15
D. 20

6. 10 + 9 =

A. 2
B. 25
C. 19
D. 18

7. 18 − 3 =

A. 21
B. 12
C. 10
D. 15

8. 44 + 40 =

A. 84
B. 80
C. 4
D. 14

Assessment 11 (Lessons 101–110) Name _____

1. 17 + 2 =

A. 20
B. 13
C. 21
D. 19

Use the picture graph at the bottom of the page to answer questions 2 and 3.

2. How many pictures were taken on Saturday and Sunday in all?

A. 3
B. 8
C. 4
D. 5

3. How many more pictures were taken on Friday than Saturday?

A. 4
B. 5
C. 2
D. 3

Pictures Taken

= 1 picture

Fri.

Sat.

Sun.

4. 22 – 2 =

A. 18
B. 24
C. 22
D. 20

5. 20 + 4 =

A. 24
B. 22
C. 15
D. 14

6. Shawna mailed 10 letters one day and 12 letters the next. How many letters did she mail in all?

A. 20
B. 22
C. 24
D.   2

7. Pete buys 19 boxes of cookies. He gives away 7 boxes. How many boxes of cookies does Pete have left?

A. 10
B. 12
C. 25
D. 26

8. Which sign will make the number sentence true?

35 _____ 28

A. =
B. <
C. >

Assessment 12 (Lessons 111–120)   Name _____

Use the bar graph to answer
questions 1 and 2.

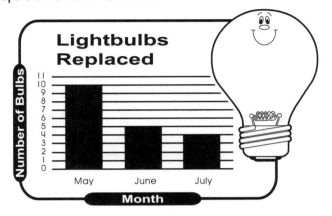

Lightbulbs Replaced

1. How many more lightbulbs were
    replaced in June than in July?

    A.   2
    B.   3
    C.   1
    D.   6

2. How many lightbulbs were
    replaced in May and July in all?

    A.   7
    B.   9
    C.   14
    D.   15

3. $19 - 7 =$

    A. 27
    B. 11
    C. 12
    D. 13

4. $16 - 13 =$

    A.   3
    B.   5
    C. 26
    D. 29

5. $9 + 8 =$

    A. 15
    B. 17
    C.   2
    D.   1

6. $12 + 6 =$

    A.   3
    B. 16
    C. 20
    D. 18

Use the picture graph to answer
questions 7 and 8.

7. How many pansies and daisies
    are in the garden altogether?

    A.   4
    B.   5
    C.   7
    D.   6

8. How many more roses than
    orchids are in the garden?

    A.   1
    B.   4
    C.   2
    D.   3

Flowers in Garden

= 1 flower

Pansies

Orchids

Daisies

Roses

115

Assessment 13 (Lessons 121–130)   Name _____

Use the bar graph to answer questions 1 and 2.

1. How many miles were driven on Tuesday and Wednesday total?

A. 7
B. 8
C. 9
D. 10

2. How many miles were driven on Wednesday and Saturday total?

A. 5
B. 1
C. 2
D. 3

3. $12 - 10 =$

A. 2
B. 4
C. 12
D. 22

4. $13 + 1 =$

A. 14
B. 15
C. 12
D. 10

5. $21 + 8 =$

A. 3
B. 13
C. 29
D. 30

6. $11 - 7 =$

A. 6
B. 1
C. 2
D. 4

7. $17 + 1 =$

A. 16
B. 18
C. 25
D. 27

8. How many rubber bands tall is the notebook?

A. 1
B. 2
C. 4
D. 6

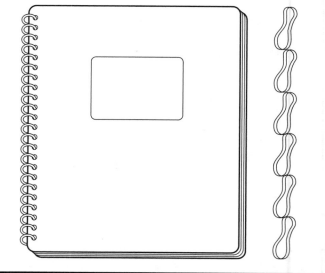

Assessment 14 (Lessons 131–140) Name _____

For questions 1 through 3, which sign will make each number sentence true?

1. 16 ____ 10

A. >
B. <
C. =

2. 22 ____ 33

A. >
B. <
C. =

3. 9 ____ 7

A. >
B. <
C. =

4. 10 + 75 =

A. 80
B. 85
C. 65
D. 100

5. Lewis traveled 10 miles on Saturday. He traveled 26 miles on Monday. How many miles did Lewis travel on Saturday and Monday combined?

A. 30
B. 46
C. 36
D. 66

6. Tonya has 8 hats. Each hat has 2 feathers in it. How many feathers are in all 8 hats together? (Hint: Draw a picture.)

A. 14   B. 12
C. 8   D. 16

7. 13 + 5 =

A. 18
B. 20
C. 4
D. 5

8. Which object will complete the pattern?

A. 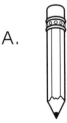   B.

C.   D.

Use the bar graph to answer questions 1 and 2.

1. How many players are on the basketball and soccer teams?

A. 21
B. 12
C. 23
D. 22

2. How many more players are on the basketball team than the baseball team?

A. 2
B. 3
C. 4
D. 6

3. $17 - 9 =$

A. 7
B. 8
C. 9
D. 11

4. $21 + 15 =$

A. 17
B. 46
C. 30
D. 36

5. Marcus wrote 5 notes. Later, he wrote 14 more notes. How many notes did Marcus write in all?

A. 20
B. 21
C. 19
D. 22

6. Sam has 19 toys. His mom gives him 1 more toy. How many toys does Sam have now?

A. 17
B. 22
C. 21
D. 20

7. $23 - 12 =$

A. 11
B. 15
C. 10
D. 9

8. Which picture shows 3 groups of 2 stars?

A. ☆ ☆ ☆
B. ☆ ☆ ☆ ☆ ☆

C. ☆ ☆ ☆ ☆ ☆ ☆
D. ☆ ☆ ☆ ☆ ☆ ☆ ☆ ☆ ☆

Assessment 16 (Lessons 151–160) Name _____

1. 12 + 15 =

A. 28
B. 27
C. 9
D. 10

2. 23 – 13 =

A. 10
B. 14
C. 16
D. 12

3. Will ordered 30 invitations. He mailed 20 invitations. How many invitations did Will have left?

A. 50
B. 10
C. 5
D. 3

4. Molly saved 13 quarters in May and 14 more in June. How many quarters did Molly save total?

A. 15
B. 20
C. 27
D. 25

5. Which square has a line of symmetry?

A.
B.
C.
D.

6. What number do the Base Ten Blocks show?

A. 36
B. 26
C. 27
D. 37

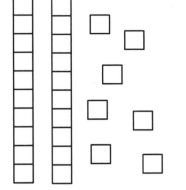

7. What number do the Base Ten Blocks show?

A. 25
B. 52
C. 62
D. 12

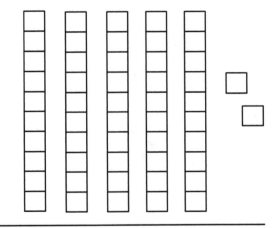

8. Which figure is most like this gift?

A.
B.

C.
D.

Assessment 17 (Lessons 161–170)   Name _____

1. What is the total of the lengths of the sides of the rectangle?

    A.   10 centimeters
    B.   12 inches
    C.   20 inches
    D.   20 centimeters

    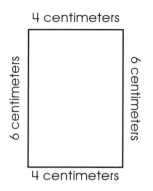

2. Which sign will make the number sentence true?
    21 _____ 28

    A.   <
    B.   >
    C.   =

3. Which sign will make the number sentence true?
    33 _____ 15

    A.   <
    B.   >
    C.   =

4. Which number should go in the blank to make the number sentence true?
    4 + _____ + 9 = 17

    A.   3   B.   5
    C.   4   D.   7

5. 21 – 11 =

    A.   4   B.   10
    C.   12   D.   13

6. If Mimi has 3 jars and each jar has 3 bugs in it, how many bugs does Mimi have in all?

    A.   12
    B.   10
    C.   8
    D.   9

7. Janelle has 29 stuffed animals. If she gives away 9 stuffed animals, how many will she have left?

    A.   20
    B.   10
    C.   12
    D.   29

8. Look at the picture. How many bricks tall is the boy?

    A.   4
    B.   9
    C.   10
    D.   12

Assessment 18 (Lessons 171–180)   Name _____

Use the picture graph to answer questions 1 and 2.

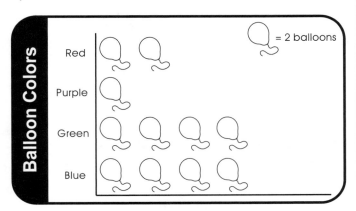

1. How many more balloons are blue than red?

A. 2
B. 8
C. 6
D. 4

2. = how many balloons?

A. 1
B. 2
C. 4
D. 5

3. 27 + 32 =

A. 27
B. 17
C. 59
D. 15

4. 68 – 42 =

A. 10
B. 15
C. 25
D. 26

5. Jay spent 28 days at camp. If it rained for 4 days, but the other days were sunny, how many days at camp were sunny?

A. 24
B. 16
C. 12
D. 18

6. Mel saw 9 frogs, 5 turtles, and 10 fish in the pond. How many frogs and fish did Mel see in all?

A. 19
B. 24
C. 15
D. 14

7. Circle the picture that shows 3 groups of 6 pencils.

A.    B.

C.   D.

8. Circle the picture that shows 10 dots divided into 2 equal groups.

A.   B.

C.   D.

Assessment Answer Keys

Assessment 1
1. A
2. A
3. A
4. C
5. A
6. D
7. A
8. B

Assessment 2
1. D
2. A
3. C
4. B
5. B
6. D
7. B
8. C

Assessment 3
1. D
2. A
3. C
4. C
5. C
6. C
7. C
8. A

Assessment 4
1. C
2. A
3. A
4. C
5. C
6. D
7. A
8. B

Assessment 5
1. B
2. B
3. A
4. B
5. D
6. B
7. C
8. A

Assessment 6
1. D
2. D
3. C
4. B
5. B
6. A
7. C
8. D

Assessment 7
1. B
2. B
3. C
4. D
5. B
6. D
7. A
8. B

Assessment 8
1. C
2. D
3. C
4. B
5. D
6. A
7. B
8. B

Assessment 9
1. A
2. D
3. D
4. B
5. C
6. B
7. C
8. C

Assessment 10
1. A
2. C
3. B
4. B
5. B
6. C
7. D
8. A

Assessment 11
1. D
2. A
3. A
4. D
5. A
6. B
7. B
8. C

Assessment 12
1. C
2. C
3. C
4. A
5. B
6. D
7. B
8. D

Assessment 13
1. B
2. D
3. A
4. A
5. C
6. D
7. B
8. D

Assessment 14
1. A
2. B
3. A
4. B
5. C
6. D
7. A
8. A

Assessment 15
1. C
2. B
3. B
4. D
5. C
6. D
7. A
8. C

Assessment 16
1. B
2. A
3. B
4. C
5. C
6. C
7. B
8. B

Assessment 17
1. D
2. A
3. B
4. C
5. B
6. D
7. A
8. C

Assessment 18
1. D
2. B
3. C
4. D
5. A
6. A
7. D
8. B

Real World Application 1

1. Write the day, date, and year on the line below.

_____

Day   Date   Year

2. Write the numbers 1 through 10 on the lines below.

_____

_____

Real World Application 2

Look around your classroom and find a pattern. On the lines below, write a sentence describing the pattern. Then, draw a picture of the pattern in the box below.

_____

Real World Application 3

Look around your classroom. Find an object that has the same shape as each shape listed below. Write the name of the object next to the shape. Share your findings with your classmates.

square _____   triangle _____

circle _____   rectangle _____

Real World Application 4

What time is it? On the clock face below, draw minute and hour hands to show what time it is now. On the line below, write the time you have drawn on the clock.

The time on the clock is _____.

2. Figure out what time it will be in 1 hour. Write that time on the line below.

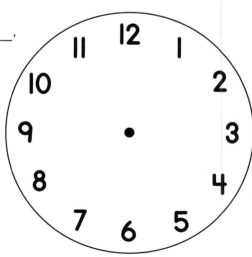

In 1 hour, the time will be _____.

Real World Application 5

Make a symmetrical heart by using the fold line as a line of symmetry. Fold a sheet of paper in half and draw one-half of a heart along the fold. Cut along the line and open at the fold. You should have a symmetrical heart!

Real World Application 6

If you wanted to give everyone in your class 2 cookies, how many cookies would you need to bring to school? Don't forget to count yourself and your teacher! Hint: Draw a picture.

I would bring _____ cookies to school.

Real World Application 7

Make up an addition word problem and write it on the lines.
Write the answer to the problem in the box below.

_____

_____

_____

Real World Application 8

Make up a subtraction word problem and write it on the lines.
Write the answer to the problem in the box below.

_____

_____

_____

Real World Application 9

Use the length of your own hand as a unit of measure. Measure the different objects below with your hand. Write the size of the different objects, measured by hands, in the blanks in the sentences below.

My desk is about _____ hands wide.

My desk is about _____ hands tall.

My leg is about _____ hands long.

My notebook is about _____ hands tall.

Now pick an object on your own and measure it.

My _____ is _____ hands _____.

Real World Application 10

Think about the number 50. What objects in your classroom might there be 50 of (such as 50 pencils, books, or crayons)? Now think about the numbers 1, 12, and 26. What objects in your classroom might you find in these numbers? List the objects on the lines below.

1: _____

12: _____

26: _____

Real World Application 11

1. Take a survey of the eye color of 10 classmates. Record your data in the tally chart.

2. Make a picture graph with your data. Give your picture graph a title.

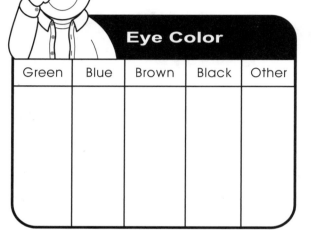

Eye Color

Green	Blue	Brown	Black	Other

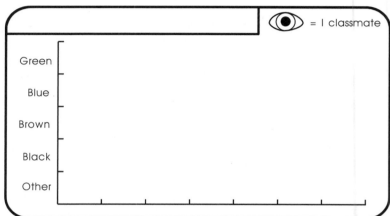

= 1 classmate

Green

Blue

Brown

Black

Other

Real World Application 12

1. Poll 10 students in your class. Ask them which of the following 3 things they like to do most: rollerblade, swim, or jump rope. Record your data in the tally chart.

2. Make a bar graph with your data. Give your bar graph a title.

Activities We Like

Rollerblade	Swim	Jump Rope

Number of Students

10
9
8
7
6
5
4
3
2
1
0

Rollerblade   Swim   Jump Rope

Activity